Fencing with Fidel and Other Tales of Life in the Foreign Service:

A Selective Memoir

By

John A. Ferch

Ambassador (ret.)

Library of Congress Cataloging-in-Publication Data
Ferch, John, Fencing with Fidel and Other Tales of Life in the Foreign Service:
A Selective Memoir, foreign affairs, diplomacy,

Summary: This memoir from Retired Ambassador John Ferch uses his career to explore the culture of Latin America and to explain the unusual pressures faced by American diplomats.

Kindle Edition

E-ISBN: 97-81939282323

Published by Miniver Press, LLC, McLean Virginia

First edition March 2013

Table of Contents

Introduction

The Foreign Service little resembles any other professional career that I know of. The work itself, where you do it, and with whom you do it have few parallels with medicine or engineering, the law or business. And that means that practically no one who joins the Foreign Service is prepared for what awaits him or her. Most probably, those who do join considered the Foreign Service no earlier than as a young adult. Few American children, perhaps other than children of Foreign Service Officers, ever look ahead and long for a career in diplomacy.

Of course you have to be educationally prepared to pass the examinations for entry into the Service. But even if those who rather late in life stumble upon this career choice accumulate more degrees than they have digits, they will still be relatively clueless about how to survive amidst all things foreign when they are first sent abroad. America is still a very provincial country, and one can only overcome provincialism through experience.

From my perspective, those experiential hurdles were a great attraction of the Service. From the first day on my first foreign assignment I had experiences that kept me saying to myself, "This would not have happened to me in Toledo, Ohio," my hometown. Many of the experiences I remember most vividly had relatively little to do with the foreign policy I was pursuing at the time. The formation and implementation of foreign policy is, of course, at the core of a Foreign Service career. And it is that policy core that keeps you committed to the career. You really do have an opportunity to influence the course of events. But discussion of foreign policy, which is the traditional diplomatic memoir, does not give the reader the flavor of life in the Foreign Service. For me, it was the more peripheral experiences and the human interaction of policy development and implementation that provided flavor.

I was in the Foreign Service for 31 years. I t was my entire adult life until I retired. I married immediately after graduation from Princeton and was in the Service that September. All but five of those years were spent abroad, always in Latin America. I served from Argentina to Mexico, in the Andes, throughout Central America and twice in the Caribbean. Although after retirement I continued working in the foreign affairs field at the CIA and at the Department of Labor, I have always considered the Foreign Service to be my career.

This is not a retelling of my career and of the times in which it was rooted: Rather, it is a "selective" memoir because it omits much of the actual work I did as an economist and executive. And I do not directly discuss the policies that shaped U.S. relations with the countries in which I served. What I have selected for inclusion are those experiences that strike me as providing insights into the peoples and cultures of Latin America, and into the personalities of diplomats themselves, including myself, insights as perceived initially by a very callow young American who, one hopes, matured as the decades passed. I have also selected many incidents in which my wife, Sue, was involved. For us, the Foreign Service definitely was a "twofer" arrangement—the Department of State got two for the price of one when they hired me and I married Sue. Sue and I shared a career.

All of the situations I describe in this memoir, no matter how strange and foreign, happened to me. I've tried to describe them accurately. But I admit to some literary license in the interest of propelling the story lines along. Because not all of the situations were equally complex, I have presented them either as full-fledged chapters or as much shorter "career snapshots."

The experiences I describe are unrelated in many senses of the word. They occurred in different countries and over a thirty-one-year period. There is no policy thread that links them together. Nor is it clear to me that together they lead to conclusions about my character development, although I will leave that judgment to the reader. Thus this memoir does not attempt to do what might be achieved in a novel or a biography. Instead, I have attempted to bring coherence to my tales by stressing the wonderful messiness of human relations and by grouping them according to the broad segments of my career: getting started, learning what sets the culture of Latin America apart, recalling some of the good and not so good times at mid-career, touching upon my totally different Washington experience, and then highlighting my executive assignments in Mexico, Cuba, and Honduras.

r a biography. Instead, I have attempted to bring coherence to my tales by stressing the wonderful messiness of human relations and by grouping them according to the broad segments of my career: getting started, learning what sets the culture of Latin America apart, recalling some of the good and not so good times at mid-career, touching upon my totally different Washington experience, and then highlighting my executive assignments in Mexico, Cuba, and Honduras.

Starting Out

It is more than a few decades ago when I started out, so the early memories are a little murky. However, a few events stand out very clearly because, even at the time, they struck me as harbingers of a career very different from those my Toledo friends and college classmates were embarking upon. The following tales are from my first two assignments during the years 1958 through 1964. They were years when I learned something about how the Foreign Service functions, and a lot about myself.

Career Snapshot: How, When, and Why It All Began

"Evelyn, please begin reading at the top of Scene VI, Act I."

I looked out the windows at the fall foliage, just beginning to peak, and thought, "Eight more months of Miss Smith's senior English." I liked English, at least I liked to read, but Miss Smith had an accountant's sense of excitement when it came to promoting her subject. It was going to be a long year.

"Hautboys and torches. Enter, and pass..."

"No, Evelyn, just start with Macbeth."

"I'm sorry, Miss Smith." Evelyn paused and tried to find the line. "It were done quickly: if the assassination..." [pause]

"Evelyn, try to be guided by the punctuation, not the end of the line."

"I'm sorry, Miss Smith."

Poor Evelyn Stempke. She couldn't read the label on an aspirin bottle without prompting. Before I could continue that thought, the squawk box squawked and the voice of the principal announced, "A representative from Princeton University is in room 122 and will be happy to talk with any seniors interested in that school." My hand shot up. I had no interest in Princeton. I barely knew where it was. In fact I had an appointment to

Annapolis and only had to pass the eye exam to be accepted. But listen to Evelyn Stempke? How aptly Shakespeare had expressed my thought: "If it were done, then 'twere well it were done quickly."

"I was hoping you'd come. The Dean has told me about you: grades, student council president, after-school work. Impressive. What are your career objectives?"

I couldn't very well answer the Princeton interviewer, "the Navy," but years of National Geographic had given me a fallback position. So I replied, "the Foreign Service." We talked about, frankly, I don't remember what. Perhaps it was the Antipodes. In any event, he gave me application forms and urged me to submit them. And I returned to "Vaulting ambition, which o'er-leaps itself..."

Five months later, after failing the Navy eye exam and having been accepted by an Ohio university that I greatly liked, I returned from school to find a bulky letter from Princeton. Acceptance and a scholarship. While I had not forgotten about Princeton, it certainly was in the far back of my mind. So I told my parents I wasn't interested. They couldn't believe it and brought in friends and family to explain the facts of life to me. So I accepted, and the trajectory of my life radically changed. A Princeton education was different. I passed the Foreign Service exam while a junior and the orals at the beginning of my senior year. And as the trite saying goes, the rest is history.

Chapter One

The only use of our attachés is that they supply their friends with exceptional tobacco.

Oscar Wilde

It was early 1959. Sue and I had graduated the previous June, married, and were in the Foreign Service. She was 21 and I was 22. Between us, our knowledge of real life could be written on a postcard. The next-youngest member of our entering class of 25 at the Foreign Service Institute was 28 years old. And out of that class, Personnel in its wisdom decided to send only us abroad. The rest were to serve their first tour in the U.S., at the Department, while we went about as far away as you can get—the last stop before Antarctica. We were in Buenos Aires, and we took it as our due rather than the bureaucratic fluke it must have been. I could hardly contain myself.

Returning to the hotel after my first day at work, I eagerly began to tell Sue about my assignment in the consular section of the embassy. I was to be the Protection and Welfare Officer. That meant that I would try to handle and, I hoped, resolve the mishmash of problems that American citizens in Argentina laid on the reception desk of their consulate. But in addition to the fact that I now had an actual job in the Foreign Service, I wanted to tell Sue about the first case I would handle.

She didn't seem impressed by my enthusiasm. She countered by bemoaning the impossibilities of her day house hunting without knowing a word of Spanish. Describing public buses driven by what she assumed were rejects from insane asylums, she complained that she had a royal headache.

Our diplomatic career was thus launched on waves of optimism and frustration. Yesterday we had stepped off the boat (in those days you could sail to post), and were met by future colleagues in the consulate, who whisked us to a hotel, gave us a bottle of Red Label, and left us to our own devices. My qualifications for a career in diplomacy were a Midwestern childhood, a lot of art history courses at an Ivy League university, three months of Spanish training, and a beautiful bride. The innocents abroad! On such foundation stones is self-confidence built.

Too newly married to understand how to temper enthusiasm and to empathize with frustration, I suggested that we go looking for one of those steak houses that underpinned Buenos Aires' reputation. Sue probably was not finished venting her feelings about thwarted house hunting but she too was hungry, so she somewhat grimly nodded assent.

As we walked through the faintly Parisian streets of Buenos Aires, I returned to my theme, reliving my first day for her, "So, after introducing me to the Argentine staff, the CG took me into his office and explained my assignment."

Sue looked at me as if I too were speaking Spanish, and asked, "The CG?"

The Consul General. The Foreign Service seems to communicate with acronyms. Anyway, the CG told me that I'm to be the Protection and Welfare Officer and asked me what I knew about the job. I hesitated a second and then decided not to bluff. "Not much beyond what they outlined at the Foreign Service Institute. I do have the job description they passed out, however." That probably wasn't the answer he hoped for, since he looked out the window for a while before he turned back to me and said, "Well, I guess it can't be helped. It's pretty much common sense, anyway."

We had reached a corner and had to stop to wait for a break in the traffic. Although all the cars seemed to date from the 1930s, there were a lot of them, and there were no stop signs or stoplights. Perhaps in the rush of old cars, the blaring horns, and the tightly packed crowds of somberly dressed pedestrians, Sue finally sensed that she was in a foreign land, for it was then that she asked about my first case. It was as if she knew, and feared, that she wouldn't like what she would hear.

So I told her how my new boss had shuffled through some papers on his desk, found a sheet from a yellow lawyer's pad, and told me, "Your first case may seem a bit unusual, but that's the Foreign Service for you."

Taking the piece of paper from his outstretched hand, I read that it was addressed to "the American consulate" and had a scrawled penciled message. It was difficult to read, but when I finally succeeded I literally was speechless. From his look, I think my reaction pleased the CG.

It was a suicide note! In the note, "Citizen X" explained that he was an importer and that Argentine customs had confiscated his shipment of TVs.

Sue had been looking at the display window of a leather goods store but she had been listening because stopped and grabbed my arm: "He killed himself for that reason? That doesn't make sense." I told her I had thought that at first, too, but the CG explained that consulate staff had found other papers in Citizen X's hotel room. It seems that the imports were smuggled goods and that he had purchased them with money from an ex-wife. Apparently the web of thwarted commercial endeavor and unorthodox financial backing had pushed Citizen X over the brink. But more interesting, although he couldn't face his ex-wife, it wasn't only because of feelings of financial or ex-conjugal guilt that he killed himself. In fact, his last thoughts were more in the nature of overwhelming anger. At the close of his suicide note Citizen X wrote:

> "I want the consulate to cremate my body and scatter the ashes on the River Plate (Río de la Plata) as a pox forever on Argentina."

Obviously, he was totally enraged that Argentine Customs had taken both his bribes and his TVs. He had been double-crossed.

By this time I had Sue's full attention and she asked. "What are you going to do tomorrow? Are you going to ship the body to his ex-wife? She may not want him."

Feeling a bit hurt that Sue had not been listening very carefully, I told her again that Citizen X wanted me to "hex" Argentina. Admitting that I couldn't do that, that no one could, I explained carefully that what I could do, indeed what I would have to do as a responsible Protection and Welfare Officer, was to carry out the first part of Citizen X's instructions. I would cremate him and scatter his ashes on the River Plate.

With that statement of resolve, we reached the restaurant that the concierge had recommended and began Sue's Spanish lessons by working down a menu listing eight types of steaks, nine different sausages, and an uncountable number of wines.

It may seem strange to Americans today, but Buenos Aires in those days had a municipal crematorium, and there was no charge for its service. So no technical or budgetary problems prevented me from carrying out Citizen X's instructions. The next morning I simply got a consulate car to take me to the crematorium so that I could identify the body and tell the cremator to proceed. In retrospect I believe it was then that my career in the Foreign Service began. It certainly was when I began to learn about survival in Latin America.

The municipal cremator was alone in his office. He was tall, beefy, and had a well-veined nose. His hair sparkled with brilliantine. In other words, his profession had not set him apart from a million other meat-and-wine-loving citizens of Buenos Aires—the Porteños—whose stylistic preferences in the late 1950s were still frozen in the late 1920s. But he was also smoking a cigar, as was I, and that was not usual. I had quickly taken advantage of the low prices on great Cuban cigars in the embassy's commissary. (This was just a few short years before a young Fidel Castro was going to put a crimp in one of my favorite weaknesses.) The cremator was smoking a poor Argentine substitute.

In my halting Spanish I bade him good morning, explained my mission, and asked to see Citizen X. He replied in the heavily accented Spanish of the Porteños, "You enjoy a good cigar, too, I see."

At least I thought that that was what he said, but I couldn't see the connection with Citizen X. More fool I! So I held my cigar up (it was, I believe, an H. Upmann), nodded affirmatively, and asked again to see the body. He looked at my cigar, winked, and led me into the cold room and chortled, "There he is, Ché."

Citizen X lay in a classic wooden coffin, wide at the shoulders and narrow at the feet and head. And where his face would be was a small glass window. I peered in intently. Peering out less intently was a middle-aged male who looked damned mad. I nodded and confirmed for the cremator, "OK, that's him. What do we do now?"

How did I identify Citizen X? I did have his passport, but that photo would have served for his entire generation. No, the answer simply was that I acted with the self-confidence of an Innocent Abroad. In any event, my new friend the cremator didn't question my judgment. He simply took hold of the coffin, which lay upon a gurney, and asked me to give him a hand.

We pushed Mr. X out of the cold room and into the crematorium proper. Set in the wall, gurney high, were two small swinging doors, below which protruded a small ladder-like shelf. The spokes being rollers, it was easy to slide the coffin off the gurney, onto the ladder and through the doors. Before the doors swung shut I saw the gaily flickering pilot light of the incinerator and felt the satisfaction that comes from doing a job according to clearly defined instructions.

The cremator wiped his hands on the sides of his pants, shook mine, and explained that I should come back the next morning. Then he reminded me not to forget the cigars.

His final remark sailing well over my head, I thanked him and went out to my car and told the driver to drop me at my hotel so I could have lunch with Sue.

"You really did that? I can't believe it. And I suppose you intend to scatter the ashes, too." Sue was neither amused nor impressed. To me at that moment it was a straightforward question about a straightforward situation so I gave her a straightforward reply:

"Of course, those were his instructions."

I could see that she was bothered but couldn't understand why. So I turned my attention to my steak. Sue, however, had stopped eating hers.

The next morning, over breakfast, we avoided the topic of the day, but my eagerness to complete my first assignment was undiminished. So I probably arrived early at the crematorium. I again bid the cremator good morning. He rose from his desk, greeted me cheerily and pushed a wooden container slightly larger than a shoebox toward me. But he kept his hand on it.

I reached for the box and thanked him. He didn't release his hold. After some moments, he said, "You are young, your Spanish is terrible, you didn't understand what I meant yesterday. So I guess I'll have to make it very clear. I want some of those great cigars you were smoking. They used to tip the executioner, why not the cremator?"

Well, you can't spell it out more clearly than that. So I said that I would be back in an hour and left him with his hand still on Citizen X. I bought a box of White Owls at the commissary (I may have been young and culturally naive but I wasn't financially stupid) and was back at the crematorium before lunch. The cremator and I exchanged boxes and probably some words, but I don't remember what. I had just had to pay for my first lesson in bilateral relations and wasn't in a mood to discuss it.

I told the driver to take me to the Costanera, Buenos Aires' riverside boulevard. We had to cross most of the city, giving me a chance both to think about my first assignment and to enjoy the great cosmopolitan setting: tree-lined streets, tasteful parks, a massive opera house—the South American Paris. The latter thoughts quickly pushed aside consideration of how I would conclude my assignment, for I was surprised when the driver pulled over to the curb. We had reached the Costanera. The sweep of the boulevard and seawall framed Buenos Aires against the endless backdrop of the sea-like River Plate. I had no specific plan, but Citizen X's instruction still rang in my mind:

> "Scatter my ashes on the River Plate as a pox forever on Argentina."

So as if anticipating that overused corporate admonition of four decades later—"Just Do It"—I got out of the car, crossed the sidewalk and climbed up on the sea wall. I started to heave the box into the Plate but heard again Citizen X: "scatter!" So I grasped the box under my left arm and with my right hand pulled back its sliding lid. There he lay, three or four pounds of small cinders. I leaned out, turned over the box, and Citizen X rained down upon the River Plate. My first assignment in the Foreign Service was successfully completed.

I could conclude this tale with an observation about personnel policy in the Department of State. Is our foreign policy really in the hands of an organization that sends youths, like I was then, abroad to do its bidding? But there is a better ending. Twenty-five years later, while chief of mission in Cuba, I told this story to the Argentine ambassador. He asked for the exact year and then mused, "Let's see. 1959. Several coups and a military uprising in the 1960s. Guerrilla warfare in the late 1960s and early 1970s. Hyperinflation and the return of Perón in the later 1970s followed by the chaotic rule of the second Mrs. Perón. A military coup again in the 1980s, and the Falklands war with Britain. I'd say that your Citizen X knew what he was doing. Perhaps I should cable the president tomorrow and recommend that he start dredging the River Plate immediately for those ashes."

Career Snapshot: First Lesson In Diplomacy

Relations between the Department of State and the American political establishment are simple to describe. You use that classic old joke. When they say, "Jump!" we ask, "How high?" Which is a simple way of explaining that an embassy "control officer" assigned to visiting Congressional or other American political delegations does not "control." He or she carries bags, runs errands, mans the bar. I first learned the trade in Argentina.

A fairly large group of U.S. governors and their wives was touring the major countries of South America. And in each country they would tour the major cities, where they would meet with local politicians. Sue and I were told by the embassy's administrative officer to accompany them and make our selves useful. We didn't feel demeaned. We were only in our early twenties, and this was a great chance to see the country. But it also turned out to be an education in some of the worst then-current American political practices. And a chance to see how a real diplomatic professional handled those practices.

The Argentine foreign ministry also sent a crew of its foreign service officers along to make sure all went well. A relatively senior officer led the Argentines; I'll call him Sr. X, because he subsequently became quite famous in hemispheric politics.

We first flew to Córdoba, a fine colonial city in the center of the country. There we saw the trip's "SOP." I should have realized it even at my age then, but didn't. It is standard operating procedure for politicians to give public addresses at every opportunity. So when we landed at the Córdoba airport, we were led into a large reception area where the governor of the province welcomed us, for twenty minutes. The senior U.S. governor thanked him, for twenty minutes. And so it went. At every stop, an Argentine politico got to speak and then an American politico got to respond. The Americans took turns; Argentine foreign service officers translated.

While flying from stop to stop and during the many receptions, Sue and I had a chance to get to know the American governors quite well. Most were fine men and great representatives of our country. Some went on to become nationally prominent politicians. But this was the late 1950s, before the civil rights upheavals that changed American society for the better. One of the Southern governors was a segregationist of the truly old school. Seated next to him on one of the legs of the trip, my Ivy-League-educated, Midwestern innocence was exposed to the dark side of institutionalized political racism.

The Southern governor's turn to speak came in Mendoza, a city in the foothills of the Andes. The highest peak in the Western Hemisphere, Aconcagua, loomed above us as we landed. The reception ceremony was held on the tarmac. Sr. X was going to translate. Our governor lit into his theme as if it were a palm-sized burr under his saddle. He was teed off by what he considered uninformed comments about racial problems in the States that he had heard from Argentines during the trip. He lambasted Argentines for their ignorance and then proved them totally informed by using words to discuss race relations that any decent editor of a small-town Southern daily would have excised in 1850. I cringed as I listened. But the Argentine audience across the tarmac had blank expressions. I then understood. Between the wind and their lack of English, they had comprehended practically nothing.

Sr. X had been taking notes and delivered his "translation" when the governor concluded. Standing next to him, I heard his every word. He gave a beautiful discourse on hemispheric brotherhood. I would have been proud to write that speech. Now there was a real diplomat.

Career Snapshot: How a Career Path Is Set

Once I had elbowed the other commuters aside and claimed a window seat for the ride out to our home in the Buenos Aires suburb of Acassuso, I pulled our personal mail from my breast pocket. The diplomatic pouch had come that day—a big event in a post at the end of the world in the early 1960s. There was a letter from a friend, another junior officer, who had met us the first day we arrived and who had held our hands while we dove into the world of Foreign Service life. As I skimmed the first page, I found that while he was enjoying his job in the Department, he was appalled by my next assignment. I started to shiver; he was telling me that my career was about to go off track after only two years.

Buenos Aires, or BA to the initiated in whose ranks Sue and I were now numbered, had been a marvelous experience. We had had great times, a daughter whom we nicknamed Ché in recognition of her exotic beginnings, and I had had two training jobs that I was proud of, one in the consulate and one in the economic section. And now I was learning that the payoff was a cul-de-sac: I had been assigned to the Department's Bureau of Intelligence and Research. While I did not know what my specific duties would be, in my naiveté—naiveté as seen, that is, by my friend—I thought that "Intelligence" meshed well with my academic and intellectual credentials.

As I read his letter I heard him speaking between the lines: "John, a job in INR goes nowhere. INR is not operational; you cannot make a name there. They will send you out again as a vice consul!" My friend, the "experienced" second tour officer, was naming the ultimate blow Personnel could hit you with. They were shoving me off the ambassadorial track. I shivered and shuddered, but read on.

Aware of how I would feel once I understood the situation, he had made contact with another friend in the Latin American affairs bureau, ARA. (Which, by the way, was an acronym that stretched back to the early World War II days : American Republics Area. The Department is not quick to change established bureaucratic ways.) This friend had informed him of a vacancy in the U.S. Mission to the Organization of American States. It was, he explained, an American embassy, even if it was occupying floor space in the Department. But more important, it was a line job; it was operational. He urged me to call his friend immediately and see if I could interest the Mission in me. Well, I had missed WWII by several years but had read enough to know the difference to a career between serving on the line and in the rear. So I resolved to call Washington first thing in the morning.

Once more my future was being shaped by my limited grasp of reality. First it was National Geographic. And now it was by a junior officer whose experience trumped mine by about 13 months. But my two years in the Foreign Service were more than enough to convince me that corridor gossip should be given more weight than official pronouncements. And the corridor said, "Personnel just wants to fill slots, not to rationally advance careers."

"Hello, this is John Ferch. I'm calling from
BA. Bob suggested I talk to you."

"Really? You were expecting my call? You've seen my file? No kidding? You were Princeton '56? Our paths must have crossed there."

And so it went, and I became the junior man on our OAS Mission, probably two steps down from the job I would have had in INR. But it all worked out, even if I had learned the wrong lesson: that the corridor always trumps Personnel. I did a decent job, and the assignment tagged me firmly as an ARA hand, a tag that I never escaped—or regretted.

Career Snapshot: The Measure of Your Worth

Well into my second year on our Mission to the Organization of American States, I was enjoying myself immensely. My job description could be summarized as "junior officer in charge of miscellaneous matters." That meant I traveled to hemispheric gatherings that no one ever heard about and whose results certainly did not make even the last page of the Washington Post. In Washington I represented the Mission on those OAS committees no one else had any interest in. Who cared? The work may not have mattered much, but I was doing it rather than passing memos around. I was a line officer. And apart from the work, I had become involved in an association of diplomatic third secretaries. So Sue and I were on the embassy party circuit. Not surprisingly, the good spirits generated by all this bubbled over and almost spoiled the show.

In my good mood I failed to see that not everyone around me was equally jovial. In fact, the secretary I shared there was deeply unhappy. One morning, after a particularly good party at the Swedish embassy, I came into the office and stopped by her desk to chat. Normally, I think I have a pretty good sense of humor. It was in remission that day, because I teased her about a sweater she was wearing. I remember it even now. Fairly large green birds were embroidered around her neck. She was a redhead. It looked to me as if those birds were pecking at an apple.

Several mornings later I was polishing a report I had written about some conference I had attended when my phone jerked me to reality:

"Mr. Ferch, the Under Secretary wants to see you right now."

"Me? This is John Ferch, I'm on the OAS Mission."

"Yes, you. According to my phone book, you're the only Ferch in the building. And I'd hurry if I were you."

The Under Secretary. I had never met him, never even seen him, except on television. The Seventh Floor, where the foreign policy moguls reside. The names up there signified power, glamour, the apex of the career. What did I have to do with all that? But I sensed questions would be out of order. So I said, "I'm on my way," hung up, grabbed my suit coat, and walked out of the office. My secretary gave me a strange look, but I didn't stop to question her.

Down the block-long corridor to the center bank of elevators. Up to the seventh floor. Through massive brass and glass doors into a reception area decorated in early Federalist style. Paintings by Sargent, Hassam, and Stuart on the walls. I asked the receptionist for directions to the Under Secretary's suite and walked into the inner sanctum. I gave my name to his secretary, and she told me to take a seat. I waited for maybe ten minutes, my apprehension growing steadily as she periodically looked over and gave me what I could only interpret as a sneer. Finally I heard: "You may go in."

He sat behind a large, elegant desk. He did not get up. Through the windows behind him, the Lincoln Memorial rose majestically.

Oriental carpets on the floor, couches and easy chairs arranged in a comer, two armchairs before his desk. He did not invite me to sit down.

He began without preamble. "Don't you ever do that again. I don't care what exactly you said and I do understand that she is probably nutty as a fruitcake. But she is irreplaceable. How many secretaries do you think want to work for an organization that is likely to send them to Ouagadougou? And you? Ivy League honors grads are a dime a dozen! Don't forget that. Now get out of here!"

He couldn't have been clearer. I had seriously erred in the field of Foreign Service personal relations. There was a lesson here that I would have to learn if I wanted to stay in the Service. And an Under Secretary had taken the time to teach me that lesson. I was seriously shaken, but in later years I was more struck that the Seventh Floor had not delegated the task of disciplining me. Someone apparently saw that I might actually have a future in the Foreign Service.

By the way, Ouagadougou is the capital of Burkina Faso, in West Africa.

Learning the Culture

When you study international relations you read a lot about the importance of cultural differences. And you pay attention because it is obvious that those differences exist and are important. And if you are headed to the Foreign Service you pay special attention. But does such study really prepare you to recognize and understand those differences when they hit you in the face? If my own experience suggests anything, you learn about cultures in the same manner you learn to ride a bike—you fall off them and get right back on. Although I was learning up to my last day in the Foreign Service, several earlier experiences during the late 1960s and early 1970s in Colombia, the Caribbean, and Central America probably were defining for me. Maybe that is because occasionally I fell rather hard in those years.

Chapter Two

Be polite, write diplomatically. Even in a declaration of war one observes the rules of politeness.

Otto von Bismarck

Someone has probably said that you learn a lot about people when you go hunting with them. I couldn't find such a quote but it must exist because I certainly learned a lot about upper-middle-class Latin American culture while 11,000 feet up in the Colombian Andes on a snipe hunt.

I had learned to hunt on the pampas of Argentina, where the upland game was so plentiful that I soon saw myself standing in Hemingway's footsteps. But for my second overseas posting I was sent to Colombia, where you actually had to hunt for the game. I sweated after likely nonexistent jaguar in jungles near the Amazon. I tried to shoot deer on the plains of the Llanos, where the deer saw you hours before you saw them. I learned a lot about what I didn't know about wildlife. Yet the hunt I just mentioned stands out, not for the wildlife, but for those who pursued it. There were five of us who used to hunt together: Ron, a political officer at the Embassy; Enrique, a young Colombian architect; Eduardo, the manager of a small brewery owned by his father; and José

María, a young surgeon who had recently opened his own clinic. We had left Bogotá before dawn. Eduardo was driving. We chatted for a while about local and American politics and then fell silent. It was going to be a long drive, two hours at least, so most of us drifted back into sleep.

The three Colombians were good examples of that country's upper middle class, at least as it was before the days of the narcotics trade. In physical appearance they looked as though they had just stepped off the galleon with Colombia's conquistador, Jiménez de Quezada. In other words, they fit Central Casting's requirements for a young Spanish male: slim, of middle height, light complexioned, straight black hair. But in more important ways they were Colombians. Proud of their professional skills, they reflected Colombia's long-held obsession with education. The sense of personal inferiority so often found in developing countries was alien to them. Superficially formal, they never lapsed into the informal "tú" so characteristic of much of the rest of Latin America. And because clothing is also a language, their attire made Brooks Brothers seem flamboyant. Thus, to the casual eye and ear they were rather stiff, but it was only a veneer over a free-wheeling Latin American soul. Suffice it to say that you could end a party before 3:00 AM only by forcing your friends out the door. These were the "teachers" who were about to put my grasp of cultural differences to the test.

After two hours on a gravel road, we climbed into the Páramo of Sumapaz, which is about 11,000 feet above sea level. The root of the word "páramo" is the same as that of "moor." But in Colombia it means a high mountain valley that is so configured to capture water-laden clouds from either the Pacific or the eastern plains. It is always raining in a páramo. Constant rain above the tree line produces conditions akin to a sub-arctic swamp. The vegetation, when you can see it through the mist, is otherworldly. Century-like plants with furry leaves spike upward seven feet. Flowers so intensely red that they seem to pulsate with electric current, but so small that four would fit on a fingernail, cluster at their base. Hummocks of moss that could have been green brain coral make walking a straight line impossible. And all this vegetation is competing for space on what little solid ground protrudes above countess ponds of coal-black water. The ponds even seem to rise up the hillsides of the valley. And the game that chooses to live in this bizarre ecological niche? A few snipe and some very scrawny rabbits. But we knew what we were getting into. We liked to hunt and this was what was available.

Enrique pulled his station wagon off the road and looked around. He told us he thought this was the place where he had hunted several years before, but admitted that the páramo all looks pretty much the same. No one argued. We climbed out , put on our gear, and loaded our shotguns. Stepping into the rain, we fanned out about 50 feet apart across the rather narrow valley.

Eduardo played sergeant and put José María and Enrique on the right flank and Ron and me in the middle, taking the left flank for himself. We started to trudge up the valley. Our objective was to—literally—kick up the game. No right-thinking snipe or rabbit is going to bolt its cozy nest at that altitude in that rain unless it absolutely has to.

Unlike many game birds, snipes won't run on the ground ahead of their pursuers. When flushed, they blast up from your feet and dart away in a corkscrew-like flight pattern. After about 75 yards they land, and sit where they land. So if you didn't bring it down when it jolted your cold, wet body and oxygen-starved brain into action, you watched where it landed and slogged over there for a second chance. So slow did our reflexes become, sometimes we had third and fourth chances. Because there was little point in making the effort if a shot was not likely; only those of us closest to where the bird landed chased after it. In this manner, our line disintegrated, but in the rain and shifting mist, that disintegration was barely evident, and we became five separate hunters.

Suddenly, I heard a sound that combined the screech of a bagpipe with the thumping of a tire that had just blown out. A blur jolted up from between my feet and then zigzagged into the mist. I threw my arms up, instinctively pulling the stock to my shoulder. With my eyes on the blur over the barrel, my finger snapped the trigger. With a burst of feathers, a bird tumbled through the rain to the ground.

It was a good shot, made at maximum distance. I congratulated myself as I walked to pick up the snipe. Retrieving it, I heard commotion beyond the next moss hummock. Reloading, I went to investigate and found Ron on the ground. I had shot him.

Appalled, I looked down at my friend, unable to react for what seemed like hours. Enrique came panting up first. He had seen Ron fall and called for José María.

I dropped down by Ron. He seemed senseless. I didn't know what to do. José María came panting up, and he did know what to do. Gently pulling Ron to a sitting position, he examined him. A dozen bees had stung the back of Ron's head; seven hornets had torn at his upper left sleeve. But José María quickly concluded that Ron was not in serious danger.

José María's words engaged the clutch of my mind from neutral to a sluggish first gear. "Not in any danger," I repeated many times. Ron was more than a colleague; he was my friend. For more than two years we had fished and hunted together. He was "Uncle Ron" to my kids. A bachelor, he would often come over Sunday afternoons for a drink and a taste of family life. You don't shoot friends like that!

José María took control. He and Eduardo lifted Ron to his feet and slung his arms over their shoulders. Ron was only stunned and was beginning to revive. Shock had not yet set in. The two of them began to slowly walk him back to the car. Enrique carried their shotguns, and I walked numbly behind. When we reached the car, they put Ron in the front seat and tried to make him as comfortable as possible.

José María stroked Ron's hand and told him to try to relax. Explaining gently that we'd go to his clinic, he promised that he would have the pellets out "in no time at all."

Ron only nodded. Now shock was setting in.

My mind shifted to second gear and stayed there. Enrique tried to engage me, assuring me that it wasn't my fault, that I couldn't have seen Ron. I heard him but it didn't really register, other than to raise doubts about his assurance. We then drove down to Bogotá, but I don't remember anything about the drive.

I began to focus again when, passing through Bogotá, we turned not to the commercial zone where I knew José María had his clinic, but to the suburb where we all lived. But I was not up to asking any questions.

Enrique drove us to Eduardo's home and told me to take Ron inside. When Eduardo, Ron, and I got out he and José María drove off. You might think that at this stage I would have asked Eduardo what was going on, but I didn't. My mind was still in second gear and not up to puzzles. Which probably was for the best, because more were to come.

By now Ron could walk without help but was still in shock and not speaking. Eduardo led us into his home, where he placed us in the den. He put a bottle of cognac and two snifters on a side table. And then he left. I began to wonder what we were waiting for, but it was too late to ask.

So there we sat in that rather elegant setting in our besmirched and bloody hunting clothes. We didn't speak. Ron couldn't. What was I to say? I drank some cognac, and then noticed the phone. Suddenly I understood that I ought to call Sue and tell her what happened. I dialed and waited as it rang. The maid was off for the weekend, and Sue must have been bathing the kids before dinner. Finally, she picked up the receiver.

"I shot Ron."

Afterward, she told me it was the voice of a seven-year-old in a state of devastated misery. She pulled the story out of me sentence-by-sentence and ended by instructing me to bring Ron home to spend the night with us. Sue too was numbed by what had happened, because she also didn't ask what we were waiting for.

Time passed. How much, I don't know. It seemed to be about an hour, and might have been, because the sun had set. And then, as if they had stage-managed it, Enrique, Eduardo, and José María came into the room within five minutes of each other.

If their departure had been puzzling, their appearance upon return was astounding. Each had showered and shaved, put on flannel trousers and tweed jackets, and as if to emphasize the informality of the occasion, tied on paisley cravats! I couldn't grasp it and didn't try—a good decision, because my lesson in Colombian culture was not yet over.

With a rather cheery, "Let's go to the clinic," José María took Ron's arm and helped him out to the car. As we drove to the clinic, our three Colombian friends chatted, about what, I don't remember. But their intention was clear: to keep Ron's numbed mind off the coming surgery.

When we reached the clinic, a nurse took Ron. José María left to scrub up. Enrique, Eduardo, and I remained in the waiting room and made small talk; at least they did. After a short while José María appeared in surgical gown, latex gloves, and face mask. "Why don't you three come into the operating room and watch?" he said. "I think that you will find it interesting."

Here was another point where you'd think I would be asking questions about what was going on, but I didn't. So we trooped after José María into the operating room.

Ron was already on the table, stripped to the waist, but with his hunting pants and boots still on. José María stepped up to the table, and Enrique, Eduardo and I played the role of observing interns. The only aspect of the scene that was not true to the Mayo

Clinic were those two English-cut tweed sport coats with cravats and my filthy hunting jacket pants and boots.

Well, José María started shooting up Ron with local anesthesia and probing for the pellets. But those pellets had made their entrance almost four hours before. The body's normal muscular activity had carried them well away from the points of entry. So José María started shooting and probing where he thought the pellets might be. Soon the operating table was a bloody mess, and the effort had yielded less than a dozen pellets.

José María stood back and contemplated his next move. I should say for the record that even at that early stage of his career, José María had a fine reputation as a surgeon and today is nationally known in Colombia. His reputation did little to clear up my confusion at that time, however.

Gently rubbing Ron's unwounded shoulder, José María told him, "I think that is the best we can do, Ron. But it doesn't really matter. With time those pellets will work their way out and, in the meantime, they wont hurt you. I'll stitch you up now and then we'll take you to John's house."

After he completed the stitching, washed off the blood, and bandaged Ron, José María helped him off the table. Ron swayed briefly, lost focus, and collapsed onto the floor. José María looked briefly embarrassed, and then checked Ron closely. "It's just loss of blood and shock. He'll be fine."

And Ron was fine, in fact. He recovered quickly. We are still friends, decades later. But the pellets never worked their way out. His barber keeps track of their movements, suggesting that they are akin to the slow circling of the planets around the sun.

I still keep in touch with Enrique, and we make sure that our paths cross every several years. But I've never had the courage to ask him why the three of them felt compelled to reconstitute themselves as weekend gentlemen before attending to Ron. But if I did, he probably couldn't answer. Their action was clearly a cultural imperative. They were Colombian professionals, and for Colombian professionals hunting attire is for the páramo, not for the city.

Career Snapshot: They Know What They Know

I was totally washed out. We had been hunting guinea hens for four hours in the scrub of the northwest of the Dominican Republic. I had become separated from my Dominican hunting buddies, had only gotten off a single shot, with no luck. I was now having lunch with two Dominican peasants we had hired to scout the birds. The temperature was probably above 90 and I was dehydrated, exhausted, and drained of any interest in continuing the fruitless pursuit. The peasants had neither an ounce of fat nor a drop of sweat on them. They chatted as they ate their sandwiches. I lay on my back for long minutes before I even opened my pack.

During the morning we had not spoken much. They just pointed when they saw a hen and loped ahead. I panted after them and rarely caught up. In any event, the dialect spoken in that part of the Dominican Republic demanded that I pay close attention if I wanted to understand half of it, and I couldn't pay any attention at all while running uphill through thorn trees. Now, as I gradually collected myself, bits and pieces of their conversation began to filter through.

"He told me he was offended because Jaime wouldn't pay for the damage his bull had done to his fence. So he went to this woman his compadre told him about, this witch, and she sold him this clay bull, about the size of my fist. She put a curse on it. Late at night last week he threw it into Jaime's corral. Jorge told me yesterday that Jaime's bull is way off his feed."

"I've heard of that woman. She has a powerful reputation. You don't want to cross her."

And so it went as I listened with increasing interest. Then they turned to me, whether out of curiosity or politeness, I don't know. They asked who I was. Since I hadn't spoken much they didn't know that I wasn't Dominican. When I replied that I was the American consul in Santiago there was no question that they were interested. I thought, "Here it comes, they're going to hit me up for a visa." Hardly any Dominican would pass by that opportunity. But rarely have I been so wrong.

"Senor Consul, do you understand what caused the problem on Apollo 13?"

They asked detailed questions about the crew of Apollo 13. They knew their names. They knew everything about the odyssey of that moon flight that had almost ended in tragedy about two weeks before the hunt. They knew more about Apollo 13 than I did!

I answered as best I could and questioned them in turn. The explanation for their knowledge of Apollo 13 turned out to be simple. They heard it on the radio. Those were the days when mass marketing of the transistor radio had pushed the price to the floor. Even Dominican dirt farmers could afford them.

But witchcraft and the space program in the same conversation? Accepted as equally true? To me those questions were mind-boggling. But for them, witchcraft and the space program were both realities. I suppose anthropologists would explain such acceptance of dual realities by pointing to the speed with which the Third World is entering the modem world. They are going too fast to jettison the past while they pick up the new. But for me, all I could think was, "You don't have conversations like this in Toledo, Ohio."

Chapter Three

I have discovered the art of deceiving diplomats.
I speak the truth and they never believe me.

Camilo Benso di Cavour

Diplomacy is a people-intensive profession. You are not only charged with trying to influence people but with finding out what they are up to. And to find out what is going on you have to go to the source. You read the press but you want to get behind those stories. Thus from your first day at a post you start trying to make "contacts." That is where the wining and dining comes in. Since the Foreign Service is a highly competitive profession (you're ranked every year and if you don't rise fast enough you are back in "Toledo"), making those contacts and finding out and reporting on what the locals are up to often becomes something more than the disinterested pursuit of the national interest

Everyone "knows" that each assignment is a potential rung on the ladder to an ambassadorial assignment, but that some rungs lead nowhere. Everyone also "knows" that if you trust Personnel to select your ladder you will end your career as consul in Nouakchott.

This is a tale of how, driven by such ambition and fueled by such corridor knowledge, I led myself during the late 1960s into a farcical but very telling cultural lesson. Near the end of what I thought was a successful tour as a macro-economist in Bogotá, Sue and I pondered the next rung on the ladder. I wanted an assignment that would allow me to demonstrate executive ability. I doubted that you could step off that final rung and into an ambassadorial office if "they" weren't confident that you could manage an embassy. But, if at all possible, I also wanted to show them that I was a great political reporter as well as a great economic one. Everyone "knew" that the political ladder reached the top most rapidly. These two criteria pointed to an assignment as principal officer of a consulate in a country where Washington was interested in what was going on outside the capital city. I didn't want to simply manage a visa mill, which is the raison d'être of most consulates. So I called friends in Washington to help me find a principal officer assignment coming open in a consulate located in the midst of a crisis in which Washington had an interest. Now that sounds very limiting, but actually there were several posts open. Remember that I am talking about the late 1960s, when the Cold War was purring along nicely and Washington saw crises on all sides.

The crisis that was closest at hand, where Spanish was spoken, and that had a consular opening in the months ahead seemed tailor-made for us. The post was Santiago de los Caballeros in the Dominican Republic. That country had been held in line for more than 30 years by Rafael Leonidas Trujillo Molina, known as Trujillo or El Jefe. He proclaimed himself "El Benefactor." Trujillo had been a favorite of senior-level cynics in the Service for many years. They said of him, "He may be a bastard, but he's our bastard," and they called him "Benny the Factor." Our bastard came to a timely or untimely end, depending upon your political inclination, in May 1961 when a small clique of Dominicans finally screwed up their courage and assassinated him. Turmoil ensued and eventually blossomed into civil war. This was just as Fidel Castro had started trying to export his revolution, so we saw his nose under the tents of every domestic squabble in Latin America.

The U.S. was not going to let the DR go the way of Cuba. Ultimately we acted on that resolve by sending in the 82nd Airborne Division to stop the civil war. But State acted even before Defense. It opened a consulate in Santiago, the second city of the DR and key to the northern heartland. Its purpose was to "listen" for rumblings of discontent and provide advance-warning reports.

Sue, the kids—we had four by now—and I sailed to the Dominican Republic from New York and then drove across the island to Santiago in the midsummer of 1967. I'm not sure what we expected in the physical sense, but to our surprise, it was a beautiful place, a small city graced with glistening new roads and parks set in the intensely cultivated Cibao Valley. Our troops had left only months before, but from the looks of the place, there was no evidence of a civil war. That observation should have hinted to me that I might have misread the signs of Santiago's alleged importance to Washington. But in my eagerness, the hint sailed right by me.

Sue and I were a true diplomatic team. I might write the reports, but she organized the intense social life that enabled me to make contacts, and she served as my intellectual sounding board. Within days of our arrival, while I was calling on the town notables, she was organizing cocktail and dinner parties. That social life provided the second missed hint that the political scene in Santiago was not as I had hoped. The Santiago notables eagerly accepted our invitations, but they came only for the party. In fact, they usually tried to stay until dawn. Try as I would, I couldn't keep a political conversation going for more than several minutes.

The third missed hint involved the mayor's explanation for the glistening new roads and parks. During the civil war, almost all Dominican imports and exports had to use north coast ports, since most of the fighting was around the port of Santo Domingo, the capital, on the south coast. The regional customs was in Santiago. What could be more natural than to keep customs receipts for local use? In retrospect I see that ideology was not a strong trait of the Santiagueros. But I missed that conclusion then.

Although several months passed, and it seemed that I struck out every time at bat, I didn't give up my efforts to demonstrate that, finally in charge of my own ship, so to speak, I could sail with the best of them. I continued trying to engage the town fathers in serious political conversation, and they responded by inviting Sue and me to Sunday pig roasts at their farms, or to beach parties. I traveled out to the other little towns in my consular district to meet their mayors, and they opened a bottle of rum. After about another three months I was getting discouraged.

I suppose that if I hadn't been so committed to a pre-identified, definitive report that would catapult me up the ladder, at this point I would have cabled the Department and told them that the Dominican civil war was over and recommended that the consulate be closed because was nothing to "listen" to. A report like that would certainly have caught Washington's attention and made my name. But, of course, that thought never crossed my mind.

It was at about that six-month mark that I read a recent embassy political section report about the revival in Santo Domingo of a political party that had lost heavily in the civil war. The report noted that the party was planning to revive itself in the hinterland and concluded that unless it succeeded there, its days on the national scene were limited. It was as if someone was pointing out that that next rung on the ladder was only inches away from my right foot. I would document the course of the party's revival in the northern hinterlands!

With that adrenalin rush I left my office to make the rounds yet again. But this time the result was not a lack of interest in things political. It was outright laughter. The Santiaguero notables thought I must be joking to even *think* that this party might be doing anything in the north. So I slunk back to the consulate, not merely discouraged, but defeated.

The consulate was in an old residence on the outskirts of Santiago. The ground floor was given over to visa operations. The Department may have opened the consulate as a listening post, but bureaucracy is a plant that flourishes in most soils, and the post by the time of this story had grown into a full-service consulate. As a consequence, my office had been displaced upstairs to what formerly was a small bedroom. As I climbed the stairs and entered this office, I saw it for what it was, or, better said, for what it was not. I saw that it was not the anteroom of an ambassadorial suite.

I sat at my desk and looked dejectedly out the window at the garden and the royal palms that marched up both sides of the long driveway. The sight of the Caribbean sun glistening on the waxen fronds and the sounds of those fronds clacking in the spring like breeze were almost always guaranteed to lift the spirits. Not today.

Soon after I sat down the phone rang. Picking up the receiver, I heard the consulate receptionist say that someone was asking to see me. She didn't know who he was, and he didn't want to tell her the purpose of his call. Normally I would have gone down to see the caller on the theory that he was a visa applicant and it would be easier to fob him off on a vice consul downstairs than it would be once he was in my office. But I needed diversion, so I told the receptionist to send him up.

A feeble knock, a pause, and a nondescript male of about 30 opened the door. Of mixed race, as are about 90 percent of all Dominicans, he was slim and of middling height. His only distinguishing feature was his front teeth; one was missing and the other was gold. Ambling into the room, he slouched into the more comfortable of the two chairs and said, "I heard you want to see me."

He had a thick regional accent, which suggested that he likely had not gone beyond the sixth grade. The combination of his self-assurance and his totally unfamiliar face perplexed me. Was he responding to my efforts to hire a janitor some months back? I see now that I had fallen into the patronizing attitude of upper-class Dominicans. More fool I.

I replied that I didn't think so and asked his name and who had said that I was looking for him.

Patiently explaining the obvious, he said that his name was José Mella, that he had been in Don Emilio's pharmacy earlier that morning and had overheard my questions about political revival in Santiago. Then he said that he was the regional director of the political party I had talked about with Don Emilio.

Mentally fast-forwarding my career prospects, I reached over the desk to grasp his hand, and began a relationship that was matched in self-interest only by the relationship Mella already had begun plotting. I offered him a cigar and questioned him about himself and party activities in Santiago. He said that he was a self-employed carpenter and that he had attended a party rally recently to pass the time. "Frankly, there weren't many others there. So when they asked if anyone was willing to do party work in Santiago, I raised my hand." I understood what he was saying. Self-employed meant unemployed in Santiago in those days and he would take any job that came along. But his motivation didn't matter. I now had a point of entry!

So I began cultivating Mella. At first I took him to lunch at the best—and only dysentery-free—restaurant in Santiago. But he clearly felt uncomfortable there. So I decided to meet him at his house. It was a typical Caribbean peasant dwelling. Up on low stilts, only two rooms, walls made of crude planks cut from the trunks of royal palms, and a thatched roof overhanging a porch. On the porch were three or four rocking chairs. No Dominican ever sits still. I'd take a bottle of rum and some cigars over in the early evening and we would rock and talk politics.

It was then that the fourth hint passed me by. Mella's conversation consisted mostly of questions about what his political party was doing in Santo Domingo, the capital. His response to my questions about party activity in Santiago was always vague. He did seem to agree with my observations about what constitutes successful political organizational activity, and days later would casually mention that the party was engaged in similar activity. But he never responded to my suggestion that we go together to a party meeting.

While our mutual cultivation was going on, I mentally was sketching out the report I was going to write. "A battered political party rebounds on strategy and tactics conceived by a political natural unknown to the Santiaguero elite." All I needed to finish my opus were examples of grassroots party activity that I had personally observed.

Contemplating my certain success as a political reporter put me in a fine fettle. Sue noticed, of course. "My love," she purred, "you really should tell me when you take on a Dominican mistress."

Sue's sense of humor takes some getting used to. I had told her of Mella before but now spelled out how I planned to impress the ambassador and Washington with a definitive report. Her response surprised me: "I'd be careful about what achievements you attribute to Mella. He's the least likely looking, speaking, or acting political leader I've seen in four tours. Make sure of your facts before you send that report in."

Sue's warning bounced right by me, diverted by my eager enthusiasm. But in the end, it didn't really matter. Mella made his move before I made mine. He telephoned me at the consulate the next day, asking if he could come out that morning. I responded as nonchalantly as I could manage, telling him I'd be free until noon. As I hung up the phone, I swiveled the chair around to view the entire room. "It's going to be an ambassadorial anteroom," I thought proudly.

About 25 minutes later I saw a bus stop at the foot of the driveway and Mella get off. He walked briskly up the drive between the marching royal palms. I went downstairs to meet him at the door, exchanged greetings and led him up to my office, where he slouched into the most comfortable chair. Now, in most countries you don't plunge right into the red meat of your conversation. You skate around first with questions about family and friends, or comments about innocuous recent developments. It certainly is no different in Latin America. So I glided out onto the rink and chatted for the obligatory several minutes. As I did so I noticed that Mella seemed to be distractedly playing with his hands. When his hand play really caught my attention, I paused. Mella coughed and keeping his eyes on his hands said, "Please, don't stop talking, Juan."

He then held up his left hand, palm facing me about a foot in front of my face. I suppose I recoiled a bit; I certainly recall being totally disconcerted. Mella didn't say anything; he just waved that palm gently in front of my eyes. Outside, the royal palms swayed and glistened in the Caribbean sun.

When my eyes brought their focal point down to the one-foot range, I saw that Mella had been writing on that palm with a ballpoint pen. And what he had written was as Dominican as the sun on the palms outside my window, and as Dominican as using national customs receipts to build Santiago parks:

15 friends need visas

15 X $350 = $5750

5750

2 = $2650

When I read what Mella had written on his palm, I was gripped with an almost apoplectic rage. In my rage I came directly to the heart of the issue, at least as I saw it at the time. However, it was also as if my rage had desensitized my tongue to the Spanish language. Leaping up from my chair, I screamed in English, *"You son of a bitch, I've been cultivating you. You're not supposed to cultivate me!"*

Mella leapt out of his chair and scrambled toward the door. I was right after him. Obviously he didn't understand what I had just screamed. But he clearly believed that I was going to grab him and do something horrible. Running down the steps, he put some distance between us and turned to beseech me. His face was a mix of emotions: fear, confusion, and perhaps a tiny bit of hope that he could salvage something from the exchange. "Juanito, I don't understand. Why are you so mad? We're good friends, and friends help friends."

I cursed his ancestors, this time in Spanish, and started after him again. As he ran out the door, I began to see the humor in the situation. So I yelled after him: "And you can't add or divide worth a damn!"

Not surprisingly, my screaming and his running had drawn from the visa waiting room a crowd of applicants. I saw that the incident would soon spread around town and that I had better speak for the record after having spoken for my emotions. So I yelled again after Mella but this time I talked about the sanctity of the law and the honor of the Foreign Service, but I wasn't even listening to myself.

The story was too good to hold so I drove home to tell Sue, laughing at myself most of the way. Sue was on the terrace taking in that wonderful Dominican sun and, if I remember correctly, sewing a costume for a children's party. I got a beer and pulled up a chair. She could see that I was eager to tell some tale so she put down her sewing and told me to get on with it. When I got to my English language outburst she too started laughing.

"You've got to give it to the Dominicans, John. They are a lot more pragmatic than we are. Since you can't beat them at their own game, I suggest we go to the beach and enjoy this place."

Career Snapshot: And They Pay You For This

Coming over the crest and looking at what seemed-to be a near-vertical drop into an immense alpine valley at least a thousand feet below, I shifted to second and began edging the jeep down the gravel road. The sky had that crystal blue-intensity that I've only seen during the first months of the dry season in the Guatemalan highlands. The valley below must have been several miles long and at least one across. Surrounding mountain peaks loomed at least 2,000 feet above the valley floor. And the valley and the mountains seemed totally empty, except perhaps for a circling hawk. We were in the Cuchumatanes range, probably fifty miles from the nearest town and several dozen miles from even a Mayan village.

As I eased into the valley—the road was barely more than a trail—Sue got out her binoculars and scanned ahead. "John, I think that there are people on that knoll."

Once on the valley floor, I sped up. There were clearly people on the knoll. As we approached we saw they were seven Mayan males dressed in full traje (traditional costume). And three of them were playing a marimba.

We stopped the jeep and got out. The Mayans ignored us. The three continued playing. One of the players had the milk-clouded-eyes of a blind man. Each held two rubber-tipped mallets in each hand. The twelve mallets flew over the bars. The large gourds that were the resonators shivered as if alive. The frame of the marimba, carved with flying quetzals, glistened in the sun; it was obviously new, just shellacked. The music they made seemed to fill the valley.

We watched with admiration until they reached the end of the tune. We then clambered up on the knoll to try to talk to them. It's never easy to communicate with the Mayans. Beyond the language barrier they employ reticence as a protective shield. But the blind player did admit to Sue that he spoke some Spanish. He answered questions but volunteered little.

They had been traveling for almost a week. Village leaders in Todo los Santos Cuchumatanes had sent them to purchase a marimba in San Mateo Ixtatan.

"Why there?"

"That's where they are made."

They were now carrying the marimba back to their village. Although he didn't say so, it was evident that they had stopped to play the new marimba for pure enjoyment.

With that reluctant conversation ended, the blind musician turned back to the marimba and struck several notes. His companions then followed him in a new tune. We listened for a minute or so and then walked down to the jeep. The feeling of having intruded was palpable. The Mayans ignored our departure.

As we drove away and out of the valley, we didn't say much to each other. There wasn't much to say. We both knew that we had been privileged to glimpse the real Mayan culture. And that glimpse helped explain how they had succeeded in resisting assimilation by the dominant Spanish culture for almost 500 years.

Chapter Four

One has to be careful when listening to diplomats to hear exactly what is being said.

Ted Koppel

Limited as I was to a Western Hemisphere perspective during my Foreign Service career I was never challenged by cultures famed for their opaqueness, such as those hiding behind the Hindu Kush, and thus can't discuss comparative opaqueness. Nevertheless, I would bet that the Maya of Guatemala would be in the running for the lead. Sue and I spent four years in the mid 1970s trying to get to know the Maya and only managed to gain a few insights into what motivates them. But those few suggest that behind all the cultural differences that set the Maya apart, they are driven by many of the same motivations as are we. But that was a lesson long in coming.

To outsiders the Maya seem to be a people who have rejected the core values of Western Civilization through more than 500 years of efforts to force them to assimilate. They speak to outsiders only with the greatest reluctance. They keep themselves physically apart from the Hispanicized Guatemalans. And they dress defiantly differently. And yet, the Mayas we encountered managed to convey, in a distinctly non-verbal manner, their negative views of the dominant Western culture in Guatemala.

The conquistador Pedro de Alvarado easily defeated the Mayas. But then came the hard part, as they say. Forced by the Spaniards to adopt the surface aspects of Spanish culture, the Mayas shaped those requirements to their own beliefs. They attended Mass but associated the saints with the old gods. They wore-Spanish-style pants and jackets but covered them with designs more than a thousand years old. A few learned Spanish, but all kept their own tongue too.

We had seen nothing like the Mayas in our previous assignments. So we frequently drove out to the highland villages were most of the Mayas lived, especially on market days. Tecpan had an especially good market, but you were wise to borrow a jeep to go there.

I had just passed a gang of the Indian porters going uphill on a sharp curve, using four-wheel-drive and low gear. As were we, they were going to market day in Tecpan. But they had had to walk to the bottom of the ravine, several hundred feet below, and were climbing out. They didn't look at us, much less gesture for a ride, as would have happened elsewhere in Latin America. And by this time in our Guatemalan assignment, I knew enough not to bother to offer. So we continued on to Tecpan, where we drove around until we found the public wash stands. Village women would be doing the laundry there. We were in search of folk art.

Sue: "Would anyone have huipiles that they are interested in selling?"

Village women: silence.

Sue: "Could I look at that one? It's beautiful."

Village woman: silence. But she spreads out the huipil. So we know she speaks some Spanish.

It goes on like this until we've worked our way around the circle of wash stands (which are just about the only public works in Tecpan). Finally I make an offer. The women chatter in Mayan. Then the owner of the wet huipil holds out her hand. A deal has been struck, but no one has spoken to us.

Huipiles are blouses that the Mayan women weave on back-strap looms. In my opinion they are the finest folk art in Latin America. We had started a serious collection. But the women and their huipiles are stories perhaps more interesting than the art involved.

The Mayan women clearly did not want to speak with outsiders. And the men were no different. In the marketplace the Mayans didn't even hawk their goods. They'd bargain, but the only verbal exchange that you'd get was usually numbers until they decided a deal had been reached and held out to you what they were selling. Anyone who has been hit by the cacophony that characterizes public markets in other Latin American countries would begin to ask questions. At the very least, what are these indians thinking? We did ask questions, but we couldn't ask the Mayans because they wouldn't answer.

If you talk to enough anthropologists, read their books and keep your eyes open, you begin to piece together an answer. A subordinated people, the Mayas have preserved their cultural identity by consciously keeping apart, both physically and intellectually, from the rest of Guatemalan society. As I wrote, they are reluctant even to speak to outsiders. So the idea of apartness gives you an answer of sorts, but that answer doesn't suggest what the Mayan woman who just sold you the wet huipil is actually thinking, about you or about anything else. With time the huipiles themselves and other items of hand-made clothing gave us another partial answer.

"I don't think we can keep this up, John. Look at these pants, belt, shirt, and jacket from San Martin Sacatepéquez, a complete traje (suit). Do you have any idea what I paid? Don't even guess. $150."

Now this is not a tale about matrimonial disputes over money, but in the actual event, the conversation went off in that direction for a while. When it returned I observed, "Well, it's not hard to figure out why so few men wear a complete traje."

"True, but then why do all, and you will agree that it's all, Mayan women wear full traje? Their kit and caboodle costs just as much. Although every woman weaves and embroiders her own clothes, the materials they use are not cheap."

We finally agreed upon an answer. It was never sanctioned by any anthropologist, so you have to take it for what it's worth. But it was an answer sure to delight a traditionally minded diplomat schooled in verbal interchange. Clothing for the Maya is a means of comparing their culture positively with the politically dominant, and to the Mayan way of thinking, morally inferior, culture of the white and Hispanicized Guatemalans. By wearing works of art, they demonstrate themselves to be superior. And there is a second, equally political part to the answer. The very visibility of the colorful huipiles is a defense to set themselves apart, and to make them continually aware of their apartness. They understand the capacity of the politically dominant culture to erode their own. Perhaps it is analogous to the decision of many non-believing Jews to keep kosher. But what about the men and their cheap blue jeans and tee shirts? Well, the Mayas may see themselves as a chosen people, but they are also practical. They all can't afford full traje, so let it be the women. After all, the men work off in the fields, away from most Western eyes.

Those insights into the Mayan mindset took us several years to reach. Another insight that I stumbled across hit me like an epiphany, however. Sue and I were in Chichicastenango on December 17 for the celebration of that village's patron saint. Tourists have long visited "Chichi" for its weekly market, but it is much more than a market town. Chichicastenango was a center of Mayan civilization for centuries before the Conquest, and it remains symbolically important to Mayans today. And the saint's day is especially important, for he is syncretized with an ancient god.

Throughout Mayan Guatamala in those years, and probably today, celebrations of village saints' days involved fireworks, religious processions and dances. The dances were highly stylized forms of storytelling. The dancers wore costumes that they rented, at considerable expense, from traveling theatrical suppliers. The costumes reportedly hadn't changed for more than a century and were some Mayan seamstress's idea of the clothing worn by Spanish aristocrats during the colonial period. They also wore carved wooden masks that were unique to each village and that were handed down through the generations. And it was the masks that produced my epiphany.

"Well, it's not exactly the Bolshoi. I don't think even three of the twelve are in step with the music, if you want to call it music." Sue clearly was not impressed. But I thought it was rather interesting. Twelve men had been shuffling in a vaguely circular pattern but were in fact making progress down the street toward the plaza. Three musicians followed them and worked away on a wooden drum, a flute, and a large turtle shell. You don't see turtle shells in the orchestra pit of the Bolshoi.

"I've had enough of this. A little goes a long way. I'm going back to the market. Don't take too many pictures."

I nodded, and Sue wandered off. The band banged on and the shuffling continued. Leafing through a guidebook on Mayan celebrations, I found that this dance was called the "Dance of the Twelve Apostles." There were indeed twelve, but that was the only connection I could make with the original followers of Jesus. The costumes certainly weren't biblical. So I decided to take a few more photos and then catch up with Sue.

As I was focusing, it hit me. The faces on all of the masks but one were tinted brown, and the hair was painted black. The twelfth mask was that of a white man with golden hair and a large golden mustache. It seemed too deliciously obvious to be true! I therefore waited for the dancers to pause. It was a fairly long wait; it seemed that they were going to keep up the shuffle all day. But they did finally stop, and I approached Golden Hair and asked which apostle he represented.

Sure enough, he replied, **"Judas!"**

What the Maya think about the White Man suddenly became very clear.

Chapter Five

Diplomacy is the art of restraining power.

Henry Kissinger

If you were to ask Americans for a one-word definition of the trait that best epitomizes Latin American culture, high on the list of answers would certainly be macho or machismo. The history of Latin America is the history of male bravery run rampant. Cortés burning his boats and marching up to Tenotchtlan with his handful of men to conquer the Aztec empire. Pizarro conquering the empire of the Incas with even fewer resources. San Martin and Bolivar crossing the impossibly high Andes to surprise and defeat the Spaniards. Pancho Villa's Division of the North charging on horseback into massed machine guns at Celaya. Those are the lessons that are lovingly mislearned from the Sonoran Desert to the Pampas.

Like my fellow citizens, before heading to Latin American I too had heard that machismo was a defining cultural trait of the region. But as a recent college graduate filled with lots of academic wisdom but little real life experience, I was skeptical about generalities. Almost immediately, however, I found that this particular generality had very real, and deep roots. And as I moved up the hemisphere through my assignments I encountered ever more proof that machismo does indeed epitomize the region. But then, as I approached the Rio Grande, I had an experience that suggests that machismo might just contain within itself a tempering antidote.

I've already recounted that my first post was Buenos Aires, a truly cosmopolitan city. The consulate, where I worked, was in a suite of offices over a movie theater. The only significance of that setting to my story is that it meant, after commuting by train from our home in the suburbs, I'd walk across the center of the city to the consulate through blocks of mansard-roofed buildings, past sidewalk markets and bistros, bakeries, tango bars, and everything that was not the Midwest of my recent past. And finally I'd come to the widest avenue in the Western world—"Ninth of July"—down which I strolled under flowering trees for the final three blocks. I loved it as only an unshackled Midwesterner could, and absorbed every sight, sound, and aroma.

Now at this point in its history the Queen City of the River Plate boasted a population of several million, few traffic cops, one traffic light, and no stop signs. Argentine drivers enjoyed unfettered freedom. On major avenues they drove looking neither left or right. On side streets approaching the avenues, they'd flash their lights to announce their impending presence and hurtle across with foot pressed to the gas pedal. On the impressively wide Ninth of July such practice was a guarantee for daily disaster. So I was properly cautious when crossing the avenue and thus observed in full detail the accident that triggers my first example.

I saw it coming and leapt back on the curb. A 1937 Mercedes taxi, lights flashing, hurtled out of the side street into the avenue. The Fiat 550 saw it coming but swerved not; he had the right of way.

The right front fender of the Mercedes crunched into the right rear fender of the 550. The inertia of the Mercedes was too much for the 550, which flopped over on its left side. With practically no pause, the right, now top, door of the 550 opened and the driver climbed up and out. He jumped to the ground and was met by the taxi driver. Both exploded with anger. Both screamed in unison to claim the argumentative high ground: "Soy Argentino!" "I am an Argentine!"

And they kept it up for a long minute or two. Neither sought to establish fault or liability. Neither called the cops. Neither even sought the name of the other. Both were too wrapped up in enjoying what each clearly perceived to be an assault on his sense of self. But the story didn't end there. The taxi driver made the first move. With an expressive gesture that raised doubt about the masculinity of his adversary, he turned on his heel, jumped in the Mercedes and sputtered off. Fuming, his adversary called on the crowd of onlookers to help right the 550 (I was happy to oblige) and raced off after the Mercedes. Catching up, he rammed the taxi from the rear but did not stop it, whereupon the taxi driver used the broad expanse of Avenue Ninth of July to wheel about. My last view was that of a glancing blow to the left rear fender of the 550.

Moving north, the next example comes from Colombia. My point this time involves not the action of the principal player but the reaction of his audience.

When I was serving in Colombia, a particularly nasty civil war that was simply called La Violencia was degenerating into banditry. Bandits claiming distant allegiance to the Conservative Party robbed, raped, and pillaged in the name of church and tradition. Bandits claiming distant allegiance to the Liberal Party robbed, raped, and pillaged in the name of anti-clericalism and "democracy." T he bandit protagonist of this tale had the nickname Huevos Grandes, which literally means "large eggs," but I'm sure the figurative meaning is clear to all readers. He was a Conservative.

Although supposedly quick with a gun, he wasn't overly quick upstairs, because he fell for a simple trap set by the police that involved one of his mistresses. She must have been in the pay of the police, or she was pressured into setting Huevos up, because the police surprised him almost immediately after he arrived for the tryst. Or almost surprised him, because Huevos shot the first three cops who burst through front and back doors. The police called up reinforcements, and a full-fledged battle followed. Huevos must have stashed an armory in his mistress's home, because he was able to hold off a hundred or more cops for hours. The police even brought up a cannon, but its shells went through the house as if it were made of cheese, and exploded among the neighbors.

But holding off the cops for hours is not a victory, and Huevos knew that the last shot would not be his. Thus late in the afternoon, during a pause in the firing, he yelled out (the battle was fully reported in all its details by the Bogotá press), "O.K., coppers, let's see if you are men or mice!"

He really did say exactly that. Huevos obviously was a fan of old Cagney movies. In any event, he screamed out his challenge, threw open the door, and charged out firing a tommy gun at the massed policemen. I don't know how many cops he took with him, but they definitely got him.

After five or ten steps he was Swiss cheese and fell dead to the ground. As he did, from his jacket spilled several votive cards featuring Colombia's patron saint. He was, as I said, a Conservative bandit.

As might be imagined, the entire episode, but especially the manner of its ending, was the subject of conversations throughout the country. Columbian reaction was best summed up by the nation's leading newspaper, "El Tiempo," which the next day led its editorial page with *Malo pero Macho.*

So on my second posting abroad I found that the Fourth Estate, at a very respectable level, confirmed and admired the fact of machismo as a regional cultural trait. Thus primed, as the years went by I was alert to even more entertaining or revealing examples of machismo in action.

Moving up to Central America I found that machismo may be inversely related to the size of the country. The following tale is a product of the Soccer War between El Salvador and Honduras in 1969.

The Soccer War wasn't the carnage of Viet Nam, but it was close to hell for Hondurans and Salvadorans. Thousands were killed. Tens of thousands were made refugees. Two economies were ruined. And the resulting social and economic disruption undoubtedly contributed to the guerrilla wars of the late 1970s and 80s.

The genesis of the war was a Honduran land-reform law that both divided large estates and limited the distribution of the land to Honduran citizens. The result was to uproot the

Salvadoran tenant farmers who had been working on those estates for decades. Those peasants flooded back into El Salvador. Tensions-rose, and finally the Salvadoran army invaded. Because neither army was equipped for a real war, the fighting quickly bogged down. The Organization of American States intervened and the Salvadoran army was forced to retire. More significantly, thousands of additional Salvadoran peasants were forced out of Honduras, trade between the two countries was blocked, and Salvadoran trade with Nicaragua and Costa Rica was halted because Honduras controlled a key stretch of the Pan American Highway to the south.

All this happened just before we arrived in El Salvador. From my perspective as we flew into San Salvador to begin our posting, not only was El Salvador the clear loser, but those losses should have been clear to everyone before the first shot was fired. You needed only to look at the map to reach that conclusion.

The ambassador in San Salvador, my new boss, was an old friend. Thus when I called on him my first day at work 1 felt free to ask him why Salvadoran government officials had failed to see the consequences of their decision to go to war. The ambassador replied that I had it all wrong, that the consequences had been clearly foreseen. Several days before the war started, he recounted, he had called upon the Salvadoran president, who was an army general, and attempted to dissuade him from launching the invasion. He said that he laid out for the president all of those foreseeable results of a Salvadoran invasion.

And when he finished, the president had looked out the window, allowed a long pause, turned back, and patiently explained: "Yes, we knew that all that would likely happen, but we had to act because—we are macho!"

So now I had a further example and this time at the top governmental level and, as a consequence was a firm believer in the generality. But often the personal is more telling than certified and official tales. The last example I've chosen happened in Mexico ten years later during the early 1980s. At that post I served as deputy chief of mission for three ambassadors and between their stays there were lengthy periods when I was chargé d'affairs. During those periods the security officer insisted that I be accompanied by the ambassadorial bodyguards. I wondered why I was not supposed to be a target when I was wearing my deputy chief of mission hat. But you can't win that type of argument with a security officer so I played along with the game.

The bodyguard detail consisted of four Mexicans who accompanied my driver and me in a follow car. They would begin their day at my residence, waiting by the gate for me to finish breakfast and drive to the Embassy. The four were tough-looking men who cherished their appearance. That appearance consisted of well-cut suits, totally opaque sunglasses, and an impressive display of armaments. Two men cuddled Uzis and two hefted sawed off-shotguns. And at all times all four wore 45-caliber automatic pistols stuck into their pants for a quick draw. No wimpy holsters for them. They were reminiscent of a police movie you can't quite recall.

The morning in question I had had the usual great Mexican breakfast. Finishing my coffee and savoring the lingering taste of chilaquiles and refried beans, I kissed Sue goodbye and walked contentedly down the drive to the waiting cars. Fernando, my driver, was already behind the wheel; he looked upset, but I didn't focus on that fact until later. The four guards stood by their car and called out morning greetings. I responded and bent to enter the car and—"What the hell is that?" I shouted, pointing at a puddle on the driveway about two feet across of what looked like blood. It *was* blood. I pulled the story from their reluctant lips. One of the four had been playing with his 45 and when he shoved it back into his pants, it had discharged. Fortunately for our friend, it was only a serious wound in the groin, or he would have had to say goodbye to machismo. Tying a handkerchief around the wound to halt the bleeding, he had announced to his colleagues that he would ride shotgun with them until I was safely in the Embassy and then seek a doctor. Rather than declaring him insane and dragging him to a hospital, they admired the decision of a true macho. So I declared them all insane and ordered them to take him to a hospital immediately. Fernando and I would risk the perils of Mexico City alone.

Would American cops have acted that way? I doubt it. Or at least I hope not. Once again I had found that machismo does indeed define at least part of the difference between Latin American and Anglo cultures. But after having that conclusion underscored in my own driveway, I soon afterward encountered a totally different aspect of Latin American maleness. The question, still to be answered, is whether this other aspect undercuts the generality or places it in a broader cultural perspective.

This tale is set during preparations for the arrival of my third ambassador. The time was late spring of 1981. A new ambassador's arrival, especially in a post as important as Mexico, has to be highly choreographed. He is to be met at the airport by the Chief of Protocol and the senior staff of the embassy and taken to a VIP lounge. There, pleasantries are exchanged between the new ambassador and Chief of Protocol. The embassy senior staff is introduced. Usually the new ambassador meets the press and takes a few questions. After a period of time sufficient to signal that the new ambassador views his host with great respect, the Chief of Protocol invites the new ambassador to join him in his limousine for the ride to the ambassadorial residence, where champagne toasts are the order of the day. The two then drive off flanked by a numerous and very spiffy police motorcycle escort and followed by the new ambassador's senior staff. Obviously this is not the type of ceremony that can be arranged with only a few days' notice.

Since the previous ambassador had departed more than four months before, the Mexican government was understandably eager for the arrival of his successor. The office of the Chief of Protocol in the Foreign Ministry had been calling me every few days hoping for a specific arrival date.

Finally the briefings and other preparations in Washington for the new ambassador's assignment were completed and I was called by the Mexican desk in the Department and told to advise the Chief of Protocol that May 10th was to be the arrival date. So my secretary called for an appointment and I drove through the incredible traffic to the Foreign Ministry in Tlatelolco. Riding up the elevator in the high-rise ministerial building I ran down my checklist of things that the Chief of Protocol and I had to agree upon.

But it was not to be, not just then, for when I told him that the new ambassador was arriving May 10th, he looked alarmed and exclaimed, "Oh no! He can' t come then." I was totally taken aback, and showed it. "You've been calling me every other day trying to find out when the guy is coming and now you say that he can't come on the 10th. Why not?"

"It's Mexican Mother's Day!"

And he didn't come on the 10th. Two governments rearranged very busy schedules because of mothers. That is how I learned that behind every Macho stands a Mama. I wouldn't be at all surprised that Poncho Villa delayed that deadly and totally macho charge at Celaya to visit with his Mama for a bit.

Career Snapshot: The Company You Keep

One of the great attractions of diplomatic life is the range of people you meet—colleagues and counterparts, local folk high and low, and expatriates of many stripes. From Fidel Castro to a gardener speaking a dialect that would have appalled Cervantes, I enjoyed them all. But one of the most enjoyable was the American ambassador in Bogotá in the mid-1960s. A political appointee, he respected the Service. He had a great sense of humor. And probably best of all, he shared several of my interests, especially hunting and fishing.

We were at the Laguna de la Cocha in southern Colombia, which reputedly had the best trout-fishing in the country. There were four of us: the ambassador; the air attaché; Ron, the friend I had shot; and I. The lake isn't huge, only about six or eight miles long and maybe four wide. But it is set impressively in the midst of ranges and peaks that soar vertically up from the shore perhaps as high as 3,000 feet.

To the ambassador's surprise, and perhaps disappointment—he considered himself a sportsman of high caliber—the guides told us that at La Cocha, you troll for trout; you don't fly-fish. That is, you don't if you are interested in catching any. So we signed on for two boats, and I went with the ambassador. Trolling was fine with me. I had never fully mastered the fly rod, and I had had luck trolling for trout in a lake above Bogotá. So I was equipped with a good assortment of Mepps spinners.

"That's one!" I set the hook and pulled in a two-pounder. The ambassador admired it and urged the guide to start the boat up again. "Another one! Boy, look at it jump." The ambassador looked, and cast his line out again eagerly. "Got him!" And so it went all afternoon. By the time we returned to the lodge for dinner I had caught more than thirty trout. Most were only in the two-pound range, but they had fought well. The ambassador had caught none, but he managed a façade of good humor. And over cocktails, his humor indeed did come back. We dined off my trout. Ron and the air attaché had caught only three or four.

The next morning we again set out eagerly. I was enjoying myself immensely, and the others seemed confident that my luck would be contagious. "Got one!" And so it went, until by mid-morning I probably had another twenty and the ambassador's goodwill began to fade. "John, would you let me use some of your Mepps?"

"Sure," I said, handing him several from my tackle box and deciding not to note that he already was fishing with Mepps. My Mepps calmed him for about twenty minutes.

Then, "John, change sides of the boat." No suggestion, no "What do you think?" Just an order.

And those trout just kept on hitting. I was probably approaching forty. The ambassador was grim. He uttered a few choice words now and then but stopped talking to me.

Finally, after I hauled in a two and a half pounder, it came: "I'm the ambassador, John, give me your pole!"

And the trout swam over to the formerly ambassadorial pole, line, and lure that I now held in my hand. It was extraordinary. Probably 70 of the approximately 100 trout the four of us caught were mine. But none tasted as sweet as those four words, *"Give me your pole."*

Chapter Six

My advice to any diplomat who wants a good press is to have two or three kids and a dog.

Carl Rowan

I always preferred the "foreign" in Foreign Service. I did serve in Washington, as I'll relate, but I struggled to stay abroad, usually successfully. I suppose my attitude came from being weaned on *National Geographic.* But such a career path ought to be put in perspective if this is going to be an honest memoir. My family was targeted by guerrillas. We all had tropical diseases last heard of in a Conrad novel. And there were whole years when I was convinced that Personnel operated on the principle, "Out of sight, out of mind." But those were problems, albeit serious ones at times, that never undermined our appreciation of the beauty of the Guatemalan Highlands or the intellectual thrill of the job. What really underscored the downside of service abroad was a truly calamitous trip returning from Guatemala for an assignment in the Department.

This trip could not be avoided, at least in our eyes. The Department will ship only one car between posts, and no sailboats. Sue had an MGB from which she would not part. I had a Ford station wagon that the Department had armor-plated and thus was unsalable. And we had a 420 racing sloop that we were determined to launch on our lake in northern Ontario. So we were "forced" to drive about 3,000 miles through jungle and desert, through the Old Confederacy and the Midwest, and over the Great Lakes to Ontario and then down to Washington and our next assignment at the National War College. Certainly not a very sensible means of making the transfer between Guatemala and Washington but if Administration in the Department had been more "flexible" and allowed us to ship a second car and the 420 we could have flown home and none of what follows would have happened.

"For God's sake, Ché, get that dog off my shoulder. He's drooling like a stallion called to service (which was an apt analogy, because Fledermaus, our other dog, was showing the early signs of coming into heat), and open the window. His breath is like rancid milk." Our eldest daughter replied, as agitated as I, "I'm not sure I should, Dad."

I should have asked her, "Why?" Instead I yelled, "Do it!" Whereupon came the panicked response, "Dad, stop the car! Archimedes jumped out the window."

Thus began the odyssey, only one hour out of Guatemala City. We had left on one of those mornings that made Guatemala, politics and bloody-mindedness aside, a truly prime assignment. We had assembled our caravan in the parking lot of the Hotel Camino Real. The sky was a blue of crystal clarity. Bougainvillea tumbled over walls like an iridescent waterfall. Tulip trees thrust orange globes in all directions. The temperature was a stimulating 65 degrees. If you approve of perpetual and perfect spring, you have to approve of Guatemala—again, bloody-mindedness aside. So with friends cheering us on, we assembled in a mood of high good humor. Sue and Anna, the youngest, would lead in the MGB, top down, of course. I would follow with Ché, David, the two dogs, uncounted suitcases, and the sailboat. And now, only an hour later, the good humor was beginning to lose its hold.

By the time Ché and David had chased Archimedes into a village cul-de-sac, Sue was far out of sight. Irritated by the delay but still pleasantly excited by the trip ahead, I pulled back onto the Pan American Highway and rolled north through the Guatemalan highlands, past Mayan farmers working their cornfields and through those Indian villages that had contributed so much to our enjoyment of the tour.

"Hey, Dad, that looks like Mom pulled off the side of the road ahead!" Sue was standing beside the MGB as I pulled up behind and told the kids to grab hold of the dogs and stay in the car. Assuming that she was simply waiting for us, I got out of the car and prepared to relate my tale of woe. Sue would have none of it. "I don't care if Archimedes runs after every female within a hundred miles. My car died!"

While it is never easy to get a clear, early answer from Sue when she is angry, I finally concluded that, indeed, the motor of the MGB had in fact simply stopped while the car was rolling merrily along. Being a mechanical klutz, I was not greatly optimistic about finding the cause of the problem. But I prodded widgets and pulled flidgets under the skeptical eyes of the entire family.

David finally asked with some scorn why I didn't simply push the MGB to start it. Which I did, and it did. About an hour later in the city of Quetzaltenango, Sue pulled over, stopped and waved me to follow suit. The MGB had died again. Not to worry, said I, "We're in the big city and can get it fixed." So I pushed it to a gas station down the street, which boasted a mechanic, and told him about the problem.

After about a half hour, he had many of the widgets and flidgets disconnected and lying about the shop. But he approached me with a big smile and declared that he had found the problem. "Señor, the gas filter was installed backwards and thus was not functioning properly. Ash from last week's volcanic eruption was probably going straight into the carburetor. So I cleaned the carburetor and reinstalled the filter properly."

Klutz-like, I had no choice but to accept this explanation, but the thought did cross my mind that factory-installed parts were usually put in right-end-to. However, the car did start, and thus we were soon on our way again.

From Quetzaltenango, the Pan American Highway plunges almost 5,000 feet to the Pacific coastal plain. In less than an hour you pass from spring to blazing summer. It is a spectacular stretch of road, and it keeps the adrenalin flowing. It was on this road that a bus driver, flying into space, entered Guatemalan popular history when he turned to the passengers and declared, "Have faith and be serene.

The brakes have gone!" Sue enjoyed every minute of the descent, and because she didn't have to touch the gas pedal she did not learn until she was coasting at the foot of the mountain that the motor had died, probably several yards below the crest.

As we looked at each other, sweat beginning to build in the afternoon sun and humidity, the first taste of panic twitched on both of our tongues. And panic is not the basis for sound decision making. "I'll be damned if I am going to push the MGB by hand every twenty minutes!"

With that I got back into the Ford, edged it against the rear of the MGB, and was figuratively damned. I couldn't see that the bumpers didn't mesh and that I was pushing on the trunk, which slowly caved in. But the car did start, and we rolled on into the next town.

The mechanic we found in Retalhuleu, (town motto: "Retalhuleu, the Center of the World." When no one has ever heard of you, you have to boast a bit.) was honest, even if the town fathers weren't. He didn't have the slightest idea about how to fix our problem. "But you know, señor, you always seem to be able to restart it by pushing. So I'd push on. I wouldn't recommend staying in any of our local hotels tonight."

Looking about, Sue concluded that that seemed like sensible advice; so we did push on, four hours behind schedule, to our intended first stop on the Mexican border, Tapachula. Tapachula has a great motel, which we had stayed in before, and visions of its pool and margaritas kept my temper in check as I stopped to push the MGB every ten to twenty miles.

It was ever-helpful Ché who noticed first. "Dad, look at all those cars. Did you make reservations?" And the answer was, "No, I did not."

As I walked up to the receptionist I noted that the place was crawling with sunglass-clad men with ear plugs. Security agents! "I'm sorry, sir, all rooms are booked. You see, the presidents of Mexico and Guatemala are meeting here tonight." She: twenty something, shaped like someone out of my high school dreams; gave me a fabulous smile. I didn't give a damn! No room in the inn or in any other inn short of Huixtla, sixty miles into Mexico. "So what are we going to do, my love?" asked my equally gorgeous wife between clenched teeth. There was nothing to do but to plunge on into the Mexican night. And then it started to rain.

Every ten or so miles the MGB would die and I would climb out into the rain and push it to life. But there was more life on the road that night than in that car. The rain had brought out hundreds, maybe thousands, of frogs. Some were crossing the road from left to right and others from right to left, while a few seemed to be racing me straight ahead, and winning. Sometime after midnight, exhausted and barely speaking to each other, we arrived in Huixtla. Inn accommodations in this southern Mexican metropolis were of the type that catered to traveling salesmen who travel without an expense account.

Sue objected, "Look, I know we can't go on, but look at those sheets. They haven't been washed since Easter, and they don't even cover the mattresses. They're nothing but belly bands!" She also described the toilets as we prepared for bed but her language doesn't bear repeating. Neither of us claimed to sleep that night, but exhaustion probably won out near dawn.

When morning came, soon we were waiting for the largest garage in town to open. Prepared for the worst, I watched the young Mexican mechanic attack the MGB. But to my surprise, he quickly found the problem. "Señor, I spent some time in the States, and how is it they say there? I have good news and bad news."

He laughed, and then seemed unhappy that I didn't join in. So he decided to give me the good news first. There was a small hole in the fuel pump, apparently made by a stone kicked up soon after we started the trip. In making the hole, the stone had caused the hard plastic case of the pump to explode inward, just as when a pellet from a BB gun hits a glass window. And the little chips blasted inward by the explosion bounced around and sometimes came between the rotors and the coil of the pump's electric motor. And when they did, the effect was as if you had turned off the ignition. So the good news was that we now knew the exact source of our problem.

The bad news, and the young Mexican mechanic seemed to be sincerely sorry to be the conveyor of this information, was that the problem could not be fixed in Mexico. MGBs were not sold in Mexico and thus no parts were available, anywhere south of the Rio Grande. "That's just great. What do we do now?" Sue demanded. The mechanic admired her for a moment and then shrugged.

There was only one thing we could do. I pushed that MGB the length of Mexico, from Huixtla to Brownsville.

"The eyes of Texas are upon me!" I'm sure I sang that refrain as, many days later, I led my caravan into the certified MGB dealer's garage in Brownsville and then turned the Ford toward the best hotel in town. Relief washed over me like a shower after a hard shift in a coal mine.

Unfortunately, relief was still my dominant emotion the next day after picking up the repaired MGB. Following Sue out of the rather cramped parking lot, and with my eyes figuratively on the trip ahead, I drove the Ford into a light pole, crumpling its left front fender. An augur probably would have said that the U.S. leg of our odyssey was beginning with an omen as potently negative as the one that opened the Guatemalan-Mexican leg. I merely cursed, thanked the road gods that my headlight and steering mechanism still worked, and followed quickly after Sue.

That day's itinerary was simple: Brownsville to Houston on a fine interstate highway along the Gulf of Mexico. Speeding through some of the best cattle country in Texas, under a sparkling sun that seems to be characteristic of June everywhere in the U.S., with islands of cumulus clouds rising from the Gulf on our right, memories of the recent travel nightmare seemed to quickly dim.

"Those whom the gods would destroy they first etc., etc."

"Balaamoo!"

There was no questioning that explosive sound as the Ford started to pull out of control. A blowout! "Dad, you are beginning to swear a lot." I looked at David and bit my tongue.

By the time Sue realized that I was not following her and turned around, I had the luggage out of the Ford and had found the jack. Pulling up behind, she saw that no question and no comment would be entertained. So she hung back a safe distance while the kids roasted in the Ford. When I had put on the spare, I turned to her and said that I was going to get off the interstate at the next intersection and go looking for a new spare tire. I suggested that she drive on ahead to Houston and register us at a good motel.

Seeing a good opportunity to get out of the line of fire, she readily agreed and returned to the MGB to get the maps and AAA directory. We selected a motel, and with that she sped off, even though by then my anger had dwindled to despair.

Now, changing a tire and buying a replacement in a small Texas town may not seem like material worthy of inclusion in this odyssey, and by itself it isn't. But by the time we reached our cottage in northern Ontario, I had blown out every one of the Ford's tires, including the spare. Such a pattern of perverse automotive behavior merits at least a brief mention.

In the meantime, as they say, Sue and Anna drove on to Houston and became embroiled in the afternoon rush hour traffic. While Sue slowly maneuvered the MGB through a sea of commuters and eighteen-wheelers, Anna concluded that she could hold her bladder no longer, just when the MGB was four tiers up on a maze of crossing interstate highways. Sue grabbed a jacket from behind the seat, shoved it under Anna, gave appropriate instruction, threw up her arms, and screamed. Upon hearing this a large truck driver leaned down out of his window and said, "Don't worry lady, I won't blow my horn. You'll get there."

By the time I reached our motel, Sue had checked us in. And she was frazzled. Not surprisingly, the odyssey thus far had depleted the store of rum that we had so carefully packed. So I joked a bit about our problems, trying to lighten her mood, and then announced that I would go out and locate a liquor store. Tired of pulling a boat trailer, I took the MGB and asked Dave if he would like to join me.

We found a store without too much difficulty, and I restocked our mobile liquor cabinet. The store was on a main road and had a large parking lot in front. I backed out of my parking slot and turned to enter the stream of traffic, but had to wait for an opening in the continuing evening rush hour. With every passing minute, I learned again and again that Houston's reputation as a city without public transportation was factually based.

Watching for that opening, I heard David's agitated voice: "Dad, I think that station wagon is backing straight into us."

I swiveled my head; it sure looked like it. The driver was backing out of his parking space just as I had, but showed no sign of intending to turn around. And the MGB was trapped between the rushing traffic and the station wagon. I honked the horn. The station wagon kept coming. I yelled at the driver, who was sealed in air-conditioned comfort, presumably with his radio playing the "Yellow Rose of Texas" full blast. It was a slow-motion disaster of the type that you normally see only after the fact, when they slow the film down.

The left rear corner of the Texan's bumper hit our suffering MGB just behind the right door. There was hardly any noise because of the slow speed of the impact. It was all rather like one of those tests to determine the breaking point of a steel bar. After the test had moved the MGB about four feet sideways, the Texan noticed that something was not quite right and stopped his car. We both got out and surveyed the damage.

"Ah did'n even see ya. Why did'n ya blow ya horn?" Our odyssey had so inured me by this stage that I couldn't come up with an appropriate rejoinder. I just became very practical. "Why don't you pay me cash now and we will forget about hassling with the cops?" The Texan saw the merits of that thought. "Ah think a hunnerd shud do it." And David and I limped back to the motel, where a large dent was made in the replenished bar.

From Houston we sped north to Canada with relatively few problems. The dual air filters in the MGB did catch fire, but that we placed in the category of a minor irritant. In fact, after seven weeks at our camp the entire odyssey seemed to soften in our memory. "Those whom the gods would destroy they first etc., etc." For the gods now decreed that the last stage of the odyssey would be its most traumatic.

We left camp as we arrived. Sue and Anna led in the MGB, and I followed with Ché, David, and Liz (daughter of good friends who had joined us in camp), the 420 sloop, Archimedes, and a very pregnant Fledermaus. (The odyssey had repaid part of our misery with some very graphic sex education for the kids.) For reasons that are still lost to us, Sue traveled with all of our money and I with all of our documentation. (That division of labor and our inability to recall its origin do suggest the gods were at work.) The morning was uneventful, and we lunched about 150 miles north of Toronto.

"Let me see the map, will you, Sue? I think we can make Bath, New York, today, but I'm not sure how we get around Toronto and then Niagara Falls."

"You remember, it's 400 to 401 and then the Queen Elizabeth Way until it splits, and then follow the signs," she said.

"Yeah, but I'd still like to see the map."

She gave me the map, I thought a bit grudgingly. "You don't have to get mad about it. I just want to see the map."

"You never believe me." More of the same. Then, "Keep the map! I'll meet you at the bridge in Niagara Falls." And off she and Anna went. I couldn't keep up, even if I wanted to drive that fast.

The gods had to be laughing with glee at this point because we didn't know that there are two bridges at Niagara Falls.

When I pulled up on the Canadian side just short of the bridge, I was really surprised. Sue was not there. Given her speed when we last saw her, she should have arrived long ago.

He: "Well, somehow we must have passed Mom, although I can't see how. You might as well get out and look at the Falls while we wait, kids."

She: "Well, Anna, we beat them, but that doesn't surprise me. So we'll wait here at U.S. Immigration."

And thus began eight increasingly traumatic hours.

Son: "Dad, you'd better start making some calls. It's been more than an hour."

She: "Anna, it's been more than an hour. They must have passed us. I'm going to drive onto the turnoff at Rochester."

He: "Officer, she's a good-looking blonde with a cute eight-year-old daughter in a blue MGB with Guatemalan plates. I have the registration on the car. She can't pass through U.S. Customs, so she is still in Canada."

Mountie: "Well, fortunately, sir, (Mounties are always polite) there are no reports of an accident involving a blue MGB but we'll put out a bulletin."

She: "Excuse me, but I've lost my husband. He's driving a green 1971 Ford station wagon, and I'm sure he would have come through this toll station."

Tollbooth attendant: "Snicker."

She: "He's traveling with three kids, two dogs, one of whom is pregnant and about to pop, and is towing a sailboat. And he can't have gone much further because I have all our money."

Tollbooth attendant: "Oh." Long pause.

Tollbooth attendant: "Well, I'm pretty sure he, they, haven't passed through here. I'd remember a group like that. Why don't you park over there and wait? You can use the phone if you like."

And so it went. For hours. Finally we each began calling friends, hoping for points of mutual contact. The gods made certain that we each called different friends. So nothing was gained, but a wide range of friends who that late July day learned that the Ferches were in deep, albeit hilarious, trouble. And we both consciously avoided the most logical point of mutual contact, my father, because he was over 80 years old and ill. Finally, we could avoid bothering him no longer and around ten o'clock contact was made.

That night Sue stayed in Rochester in the last room available in the midst of a Mormon convention. Not a drop to drink was to be had. I stayed in Niagara Falls, Ontario, but had only $15 scraped together from Liz and Ché. And I had to save some of that for gas. The room we found was only two steps up from a flop. The girls slept on the bed and David and I on the floor.

That is the end of the tale. We drove to Washington the next day with no additional crisis. There is no self-evident punch line to this tale. But the conclusion is fairly clear. There can be a downside to service abroad and when you are on it you had better hope that your family has a sense of humor.

Career Snapshot: In Harm's Way

The civil wars of the 1970s and 1980s in Central America were just about the last flutter of the Cold War. Of course, those civil wars weren't cold. They boiled. Perhaps more to the point, they helped shape five of my assignments. In fact, Sue and I were present at the very beginning of the crisis. But that beginning was as farcical as it was terrifying.

In 1970 we were stationed in San Salvador, where absolutely nothing seemed to be going on. I was sent to a conference in Panama and took Sue along for the shopping. Before leaving we arranged to meet friends at a concert the night of our return, which we did. An embassy colleague told us during intermission that he had heard that afternoon that a prominent Salvadoran, a Regalado, one of the infamous "fourteen families" who were said to own and run that little country, had been kidnapped. Our friend knew nothing about the kidnappers.

After the concert we invited the friends to our home for drinks. I pulled up to our driveway and got out to open the gate. "Are you Mister John Arthur?"

The question, in Spanish, came from a casually dressed young man who stepped out of the shadows by the gate. His distinguishing feature was an automatic assault rifle. A similarly armed companion stepped out behind him. My mind went into overdrive, but the clutch did not fully engage. My first thoughts were, "Regalado!" "Kidnappers!" but I didn't ask myself why I wasn't staring up the muzzle of those assault rifles. My second thoughts were, "Keep them talking while Sue and our friends run for the house." So I replied, "No, my name is not Arthur. Who are you?"

But I knew that they were looking for me. They had simply assumed my middle name was my patronymic. Moving toward them, I whispered to Sue to get in the house.

"We're from the National Guard, and we've been sent to protect you."

Sue and our friends jumped from the cars and ran to our front door. The two young men looked at each other, bewildered. I asked for their identification papers. They had none; they had "forgotten" them. They then began to talk to each other, trying to figure out what they had gotten into. I took advantage of their confusion, so I thought, to break away running to the house, where I telephoned our police liaison.

"Jess, do you know my middle name?"

"No, why?"

"You'd better get the hell over here, fast."

Jess came and calmed us all down. He knew the guardsmen, for they were that, but he didn't know why they were sent, or why I needed "protection."

So the next day I went directly to the ambassador's office and asked if he knew what was going on. He did indeed, because he had requested the National Guard to provide protection. He regretted that events had been so tumultuous that he had "forgotten" to give me warning, but then he passed me a copy of a letter. It was the letter the kidnappers had sent to the Regalado family. It concluded:

"And to prove that we have him we are enclosing the business cards of his little friends and co-magnates found in his wallet. Beginning with John Arthur Ferch."

I had been launched in "harm's way" on waves of forgetfulness.

Career Snapshot: Corporate Culture

The Foreign Service brings its officers back occasionally to staff out the Department of State. For most of my career, as I have said, I avoided such assignments. But then, many of my colleagues preferred them. It takes all kinds.... But perhaps the Department has reasons for such an assignment policy. I have to admit that I learned more about my country during those few years that I did serve in Washington than I ever did while abroad.

I first became fully aware that different corporate cultures exist within the U.S. Government, and thus that the Foreign Service might have its own unique mores, when I was assigned to the National War College for senior training. Three-quarters of the students were from the military services, and all of those were tagged as future generals and admirals. But that is all they had in common. Each service had a culture as distinct as its uniforms. In fact, even when in civilian clothes they were still "in uniform." The Air Force favored flashy sport coats; the Navy shopped at Brooks Brothers, and, dare I say it, the Army was clad in polyester. And those of us from the Foreign Service? Well, as I previously said, I originally wanted to be a naval officer. I now found that I would have fit right in.

After that year, I assumed that I would go back to Latin American affairs, and struggled to do so. However, the powers that be thought otherwise, and I was sent to the

Bureau of Economic and Business Affairs as an office director in charge of international agricultural policy. If organization charts were honestly labeled, that office would have been designated a liaison with the Department of Agriculture, since that bureaucracy really has the last say in international agricultural policy.

Anyway, there I was, and I had to make the best of it. So that first week, I got a cab and rode up Constitution Avenue and over to Independence Avenue to the Department of Agriculture to introduce myself. And was taken in to meet the Secretary of Agriculture! Seventeen years in the Foreign Service, and I had only met a Secretary of State several times, and then only in very formal settings. After chatting a bit, the Secretary of Agriculture said, "Well, John, it' about time for lunch. Let's go down to the cafeteria and get a sandwich." I could barely respond, I was so surprised. So we went to the cafeteria, the first of many such lunches with the Secretary. The entire Department of Agriculture was so informal you half expected someone in bib overalls to bump into you coming around a corner in the halls and say, "Ah, shucks, I'm really sorry."

For a Midwesterner, it was a delightful experience. I still aspired to be called "Mr. Ambassador," but there was certainly something attractive about this totally different corporate culture. However, getting on a first-name basis with the Secretary of Agriculture also led to a minor disaster for our family budget. The disaster began just before a meeting of very senior Department of Agriculture officials convened to consider the position the United States would adopt at the annual meeting of the U.N.'s Food and

Agricultural Organization. While we were waiting for several stragglers, someone mentioned the moaning and groaning that low beef prices were generating among ranchers. "They'll be happy again, soon enough," the Secretary observed. "Prices are at rock bottom right now and will start back up any day. Hey, I told my wife last night that she ought to buy as much beef as she can cram in the freezer this weekend."

"Sue, those were his very words. The Secretary said that this is a historic low and it won't last. We have to take advantage of it."

So, you guessed it. We went to Sears that evening and bought the largest freezer in stock. And that weekend Sue filled it with beef cuts of all sorts at "rock bottom" prices.

And you probably guessed it again. For the next six months beef prices continued to weaken until they were probably 50 percent below "rock bottom." At least in the corporate culture of the State Department, no one ever suggests that you buy Ecuadoran banana futures because there is going to be a coup and prices will break through the ceiling.

Chapter Seven

What is the difference between the diplomat and the military man? They both do nothing, but the military get up very early in the morning to do it with great discipline, while diplomats do in the late afternoon, in utter confusion.

Vernon A. Walters

Given my own enthusiasm for the job it has always surprised me how little respect, much less affection, Americans have for their diplomats. "Striped pants boys" was Truman's observation. Jack Kennedy said that the "State Department is a bowl of jelly." There are other quotes in the same vein that I've tried to forget. The contrast between such views and the public's attitude toward our military could not be greater. That ought to be a surprise also, because I will lay odds that more American ambassadors have been killed on duty during my career than were American generals and admirals. If you are in the Foreign Service, the public's vague antipathy can be moderately irritating, but usually it is an academic irritation because it doesn't touch you directly. Once, however, it did, and for a brief time I became infamous to some of my fellow citizens.

During my tour as office director in charge of international agricultural policy I had an enormous amount of contact with the American public. I was given that job because of one of Henry Kissinger's few interventions into Foreign Service personnel policy. About the time that I was finishing my year at the National War College, he decreed that every FSO had to have experience in several regions. He further said that if an officer had thus far specialized in a single region, as I had done, on his next assignment he had to move into the unknown. There were a lot of rumors floating through the corridors about why he did this, but the gist of most seemed to be that he found us to be a bit parochial.

I knew that my assignment would be in the Department, because I had been in the field for 12 years. But I wanted to stay with Latin American affairs. It wasn't to be. Personnel interpreted Kissinger's policy to mean that musical chairs had to be played within the Department as well as among posts. So they sent me for a job interview with the Assistant Secretary for Economic and Business Affairs.

He became, subsequently, one of my heroes for his effectiveness in furthering U.S. economic interests. But what I remember from that interview was his question about whether I was willing to do a lot of public speaking all over the place. It seems that during the previous year or so agricultural matters, and food particularly, had become contentious international issues. And in the most convoluted manner I could imagine.

OPEC had only recently burst on the scene with its price hikes. It wasn't long before there was a ballroom full of wannabe cartel-makers dancing us ragged. Bananas, tropical timber, coffee, you name it and some group thought that their hopes for a happy and prosperous future were at hand. So the "South"—the developing countries—organized in order to pressure the "North"— the developed countries—to accept cartels. (The South knew that they would all cheat if they tried to control exports in order to make a cartel work, so they reasoned that the only effective procedure would be for the North to limit imports.) And then there were several poor harvests spread rather widely around the globe. The South, now organized, seized that issue and demanded a World Food Conference to gain commitments from the North to feed their hungry. And that demand resonated among many sectors in the North. And in the midst of all this the Soviets cornered our wheat market. The story up to this point—I perhaps became a bit cynical—is that the U.S. Government was confronting demands to jack up the price of bananas, solve the problem of world hunger, and get a handle on a Soviet Union that had learned to play the commodities market. And while this was going on, for totally unrelated reasons the farm sector in the U.S. was in recession. And do you suppose that American farmers also didn't demand U.S. Government support? To make sure that they got the government's attention, they periodically drove their tractors and combines into Washington at rush hour.

It was this mishmash of issues and pressure groups that was on the Assistant Secretary's mind when he asked if I was a willing public speaker. He wanted the Department to defend itself, or at least to convince the disgruntled that it was doing something. The problem, or I should say problems, was both that the Department had relatively little ability to do much about any of the problems and that remedies for one problem probably would undercut solutions for others. The classic example was food aid to the hungry in the Third World; such aid depressed prices and thereby undercut our other, and unrelated, efforts to help Third World farmers increase production.

Pushing those inconvenient thoughts aside, I got up to speed on the issues and policies and began to juggle the incoming speaking invitations. Monday I'd assure the farmers of Des Moines that our top priority was to persuade the European Community to open their agricultural market. Tuesday I'd assure Canadian and Australian officials that we certainly would not undercut their wheat exports with our food aid giveaways. Wednesday I'd promise the Quakers that our goal was to prevent a single hungry belly in the Horn of Africa. Thursday I'd explain to a local Council on Foreign Relations how we were managing the Soviets. And on Friday I'd get on a plane and go to some international gathering where I would speak "diplolingo" to fuzzy up our policy on commodity cartels.

At the time I remember longing to deal once again with those straightforward, corrupt Latin American politicians with whom I had become so familiar, and perhaps so comfortable. But I didn't have a choice, so I stayed on the merry-go-round for two years. And toward the end of that period something happened that catapulted me towards infamy: *I began to be believed!*

All of this public speaking seemed to have caught the attention of the staff of *Southern Farmer,* a publication whose reach I soon found extends far beyond the Old Confederacy. The tractorcades were again amusing the broader American public and infuriating Washington commuters. So *Southern Farmer* decided to put a bureaucratic face on the source of the farmers' anger. As I said, they had heard of me and asked for an interview. I gave them my various spiels, trying to blur over the contradictions. And soon I appeared as a lead article, "Four Who Can Make or Break Farm Prices."

And beneath that headline, my smiling face, along with three colleagues from the Department of Agriculture, peered out at the farm audience. A politically agitated sector of the American public was being told that the Department of State, in the person of one middle-ranking, middle-aged FSO, was relevant to their interests. And they didn't like it one bit!

The calls and telegrams began that day, the letters soon after. The mailroom in the Department set up a special drop box for my office. Farm wives called Sue. I remember one particular letter signed by about 50 farm wives from Kansas. They listed their husbands' crops and acreage. Collectively their holdings approached the size of a smallish European country. I still don't understand why they took that route if they wanted my sympathy. I was tempted to respond by describing my mortgaged half acre.

I had done my job. I did what the Assistant Secretary wanted. But the result wasn't what he had anticipated. The

Department was now hoist on its own petard, and you spell "petard" f-e-r-c-h. A really fine gentleman, the Assistant Secretary laughed it off by acknowledging that the Department couldn't even make or break prices in its cafeteria.

A large sector of the American public had been told that that just wasn't true, by a publication it trusted. So, although my back was covered in the Department, my face continued for some months to raise the ire of the farm community. The Foreign Service had once again lost a battle of public relations. However, perhaps it was our own fault, at least partially. As I explained earlier, we had little ability to influence most of the problems I was charged to handle. It was as if I had been dealt a pair of threes in a poker game and told to bluff it out.

Career High Points

The question most commonly heard by Foreign Service Officers when asked about their careers is, almost certainly, "Which was your favorite post?" The answer cannot be so simply put, however, because not only is every post different but you serve in each at a different time in your life, family, and career. We enjoyed all of our posts but for widely different reasons. For example, it would be hard to find a more perfect post for a young family than El Salvador with its fine climate and beaches. And Guatemala offers the very best in Latin American tourism. But the posts that really stand out are those that combine personal enjoyment with professional challenge. For us those posts were Mexico, Cuba, and Honduras.

Few countries are as complex and as important to the United States as is Mexico. Today Mexico and the United States are intimately intertwined economically through the North American Free Trade Agreement. But even when I served there in the late 1970s and early 1980s Mexico was our third largest trading partner and Mexican emigration to the United States was reshaping our cultural landscape. And at that time, as if to make sure that our diplomats earned their pay, the foreign policies of the two governments jostled each other rather than marched in step. Stir in a wonderfully different culture and a very prickly sense of nationalism and you had the makings of a great assignment.

Chapter Eight

The two maxims of any great man at court are, always to keep his countenance and never to keep his word.

Jonathan Swift

Because diplomats are always conscious, at least they should be, of the national interests at stake in the country of their assignment, they like to think that they pursue those interests in a rational manner. You don't get paid to recommend an emotionally driven policy. Now this obviously isn't always the case, but you do try to be rational. And because you do, you also usually ascribe rationality to your counterparts in the host government. While serving as Deputy Chief of Mission in Mexico during the late 1970s I tripped over such assumptions and learned thereby that diplomacy can be as irrational as any other interaction between human beings. It all happened when the ambassador was out of the country, a fact that left me in charge of the embassy, the chargé d'affairs a.i. (ad interim, meaning temporary.)

"John, the Deputy Secretary is on the secure phone."

There was only the least hint of excitement in my secretary's voice. Totally confident of her ability to dominate the 600-some employees of our embassy in Mexico City, she would have fallen on her stenographer's pencil before admitting that a secure call from the Deputy Secretary of State to a mere chargé d'affaires was not a routine occurrence. Not to appear less blasé than she, I broke away from contemplating Chapultepec Castle, which towered outside my window above the smog of the Paseo de la Reforma, and walked casually to the secure room in which sat our secure telephone. Diplomacy had come a long way from the day when a Secretary of State rejected clandestinely gathered information, explaining that gentlemen do not read the mail of other gentlemen.

I picked up the phone and started to utter the ritualistic banalities of opening conversational gambits in the Foreign Service only to be cut off by an unexpectedly nervous voice.

"John, the Shah [of Iran] will return to Mexico on Tuesday, and I want you to immediately advise the Foreign Minister of the Shah's return. Now, I know that you don't know any of the background about why he left, and there is no time to brief you. But you do know that there has been hell to pay since those Iranian students took over our embassy, and you can fill in the details for yourself."

With that he hung up, and I tried to "fill in" the rationale of our policy while my secretary sought an immediate appointment with the Foreign Minister. He was out of town, so she had to settle for the Deputy Foreign Minister, which was appropriate, I mused, since he probably was as much in the dark as I was about the circumstances under which the Shah had left Mexico. About all I knew was that the Shah of Iran had been dethroned by a revolution led by Muslim fundamentalist clerics. That those fundamentalists didn't like the West and particularly didn't like the United States. That Iranian students, egged on by the fundamentalist clergy, had invaded our embassy in Teheran and were holding our diplomats hostage.

While in the National War College, I had traveled to Iran and met the Shah and, as a consequence, was personally host to radically conflicting emotions. I had a real sympathy for anyone opposed to the Shah. He had struck me as a megalomaniac. But how dare they take my colleagues hostage? That cut too close to the bone. However, beyond those few facts and feelings, I really didn't know anything about the Iranian revolution and our role in supporting the Shah's flight. And I certainly didn't know what role Mexico was playing in all this. The Shah's arrival in Mexico some months before this phone call had been handled personally by the Ambassador, and, under instructions from Washington, he had shared that development with no one in the embassy.

While my chauffeur battled Mexico City's near-permanent gridlock, I tried to construct a presentation around the two facts I had been given: a) the Shah is returning; b) on Tuesday—and came up empty.

It didn't matter. After engaging in the usual chitchat, when I laid those two facts metaphorically on his desk, the Deputy

Foreign Minister jumped out of his chair and exclaimed, "Oh my God, what is going to happen to our embassies?"

I recall thinking that that was a pretty good point, even if it wasn't phrased in the diplo-speak of national interests. But I couldn't commiserate, of course, and in any event the Deputy Foreign Minister was running to the door. My meeting was over.

But the game was just beginning. No sooner had I returned to the embassy than the Deputy Foreign Minister's secretary called me and explained that he had told her to read me a statement that he had just released to the press: 'The Shah has asked to return to Mexico. The Mexican authorities have denied his request."

Thus far the story is a simple one since it involves only two declarative sentences: "He's coming." "He's not." Diplomacy is not always burdened with a lot of rhetoric. But rhetoric was on the way.

When I called the Deputy Secretary to report my conversation and the Mexican press release, he thanked me and hung up, leaving me as much in the dark as I was before his first call. Others in Washington were not so tight-lipped. Through press reporting the next day of conversations with "high officials who prefer to remain unnamed," I learned that the Shah, before leaving Mexico, had been given the written and personal promise of the President of Mexico that he would always be welcome in Mexico should he wish to return. Some in Washington obviously felt that we had been stabbed in the back by perfidious Mexico, and they were determined to let the world know about this act of treachery. And when they did, the Mexicans were equally furious that presidential correspondence had been released. The Foreign Ministry formally denied that any presidential promise had been made. And from such continuing exchanges, all, or almost all, of the facts came out.

After the Iranian revolution, while the exiled Shah was flying hither and yon seeking a friendly government that would allow him appropriately comfortable refuge, prominent Americans exerted influence to secure a landing in Mexico. They felt that they "owed" him, but they didn't want him in the U.S. Then, when the Shah's health deteriorated, prominent Americans, probably the same ones, persuaded our government that we owed the Shah medical treatment in the U.S. Before the Shah made the move, however, someone, probably within that group of prominent Americans, was foresighted enough to persuade the Mexican president that he should extend to the Shah the promise that he would always have a home in Mexico.

The promise was quickly needed, because it was the Shah's presence in the U.S. that ostensibly provoked the Iranian students to occupy our embassy in Teheran and make hostages of our diplomats there. At that point we apparently decided that we had paid enough of our debt to the Shah, and the Deputy Secretary called me.

The evening after the rhetorical salvos fired by Washington and Mexico City, Sue and I were home having a drink before dinner. I wanted to share my emerging interpretation of the manner in which both we and the Mexicans were handling the set to. "Quite a flap, no? Who ever thought Mexico would be part of the Iranian mess? But I tell you, what I find interesting is that no one, no politician, no press pundit, has focused on how typical it is of Mexican-American relations."

Sue looked up from the paper she was reading and raised her eyebrows, preparatory to listening to a lecture. She put down the paper. "OK, you win, tell me about 1847 again."

Now that threw me off stride because I was going to begin with Santa Ana and Winfield Scott, the fall of Chapultepec Castle and the martyrdom of the Child Heroes to explain how both sides, inevitably, screwed up again, because we never remember and they never forget. But my wife, who had learned U.S.-Latin American relations by my side during the previous twenty-five years, had just denied me the opportunity to start again at chapter one.

So I regretfully told her to skip the preamble and to ask herself two questions: Why did Washington think that if the Shah was too hot for us to handle, the Mexicans would be happy to have him back? Second, why didn't the Mexicans realize that relations with the U.S. are too important to be conducted through press releases, that their interests would have been better served by saying "no" privately and giving us a few days to find another landing for the Shah?

Well, obviously neither she nor I had any answers to that question, and so Sue returned to her paper and I picked up a book. But in time an answer did come.

Almost a year had passed and the Shah and the Iranian crisis were history. I was again chargé d'affaires. A very prominent American senator was in Mexico on an official visit. We were in my office where, preparatory to meeting the Foreign Minister, I had briefed him on all of the many and ever- changing issues that bedevil Mexican-U.S. relations. After I finished, the senator had stood up and looked out the window at Chapultepec Castle. Observing that we had a bit of time before we had to battle our way through traffic to the Foreign Ministry, and saying something about the burden of history that the Castle carried, I asked him if he'd be willing to listen to a bit of more recent history. I added that, if he was so inclined, he could help me obtain some answers raised by those recent developments.

The *s*enator was a man of international prominence and ideally suited for my purpose. As I related the history of the Shah's non-return to Mexico and then suggested how I thought Mexico should have acted if it had kept the full range of its interests in mind, he nodded understanding and agreed to raise the issue with the Foreign Minister.

So the meeting was held. While I participated largely as an observer, the skilled politician and the able diplomatist conducted a tour d'horizon of hemispheric and world developments. They clearly respected each other and had little difficulty reaching broad agreement on many issues. When the agenda of the moment was covered, the senator leaned over, touched the foreign minister on the knee as if to pass on a confidence, and said, "It is regrettable that all too often our governments fail to achieve such understandings as we have. Obviously, it's easier for me to see why we Americans so often act against what in retrospect is our mutual interest. Mexican motivations, however, are not usually so clear to me. With your permission I'd like to ask you about a misunderstanding last year."

The Foreign Minister obviously had been charmed by the senator and readily agreed. The senator then retold the sad episode at the core of this tale with such artistry that the merits of both positions became self-evident. He dealt so tactfully with the issue of the presidential promise and subsequent denial that the Foreign Minister readily agreed with the facts as presented. The senator then concluded with my question: "Why didn't you tell us 'no' privately and then give us time to find another port for the Shah?"

The Foreign Minister leaned his long body back into his chair, closed his eyes as if in deepest thought, and then came forward gracefully as if to suggest a physical parallel to the intellectual concept he was about to expound. Eyes met, a smile was briefly offered, and then he chuckled, "We never said we were consistent."

And that was that. Some appropriate reply might have been possible, but the senator and I were both too astounded by the Foreign Minister's declaration to attempt one. So we made our goodbyes and walked to our car past the Aztec and colonial buildings on the Ministry's grounds that serve as symbols of the relevance of Mexico's past to its current foreign policy, and burst out laughing.

The senator repeated several times what the Foreign Minister had said: "We never said we were consistent." He then clapped me on the back and said that he had never heard such a wonderful admission of irrationality.

It was then that it came to me. I stopped walking, turned to him and explained, "Senator, there is a great local expression that may explain it all: *Como Mexico No Hay Dos,* which figuratively translates as 'There is only one Mexico, there can't be another place like it.' It's usually said in recognition of some screw -up. But you know, I wonder about how unique they are in the field of screw-ups."

He nodded, whispered, "Only in America," and closed the subject.

Career Snapshot: Democratic Diplomacy—An Oxymoron?

"Fernando, it's an appointment with the president. We're late. You've got to find a way to cut through this mess."

He couldn't. No one could. And I was late. I was delivering a message from our president to the Mexican president giving him advance notice that the United States was going to recognize China. That's Communist China, Nixon and Kissinger's great coup. And I was stuck in Mexico City traffic. No one in Washington laughed.

Twenty million people. It seemed that 19 million of them were always in front of you. Mexico City, one of the great cities of the world, that is, if you could cross the street. Mexico City, one of the most fascinating and intellectually challenging posts in the Foreign Service, if that you could *get* to work. Six hundred-plus members of the embassy staff, about half Americans and half Mexicans. And one subject of conversation—the incredibly awful traffic.

"John, you are chargé d'affaires now, probably for the next four months, at least. You're in command. Change the embassy hours so that we miss the worst of the rush hours. The Department won't care. They'll probably applaud your initiative."

"So you say. But for the sake of argument, what hours do you propose?"

And so the conversations went. I sympathized with my colleagues. I had a driver and they didn't. And even for me, traffic was a pain in the neck. But I also saw that I was never going to please all of my fellow workers because their own schedules varied so greatly. That was because Mexican government offices, and thus my colleagues' counterparts, kept wildly different hours. The more traditional ones, including the foreign ministry, even pretended that nothing had changed since Mexican independence in 1820, when the city had fewer than several hundred thousand inhabitants and the siesta ruled the day. They started work at 10:00, broke at 3:00 for three or four hours, and returned to work until 8:00 or 9:00. If my colleagues who dealt with such ministries worked from eight until five, they'd barely overlap their counterparts. But if we kept foreign ministry time, they'd barely overlap their families.

Our Mexican employees also complained. Most used public transportation. The scene there was so bad that the city's subway system had all-male and all-female cars during rush hours.

So I was badgered from all sides and gradually was being worn down. Finally the idea came. I represented the world's oldest functioning democracy. What could be more appropriate than voting on embassy hours? Every one of the six hundred-plus employees would have a say. Maybe a clear preference would emerge, and I would be off the hook.

So my secretary printed up ballots and sent them around. The ballots suggested various possible times but also allowed for a write- in vote.

As my secretary and I counted the returns, it became evident that I had made a life-threatening error. Almost all of the 300 Mexican employees had voted as a bloc. Most of them never had to leave the embassy during the day. Their problem was only rush hour, and they wanted to avoid it by coming in at 6:30 AM, take no lunch hour, and leave at 2:30 PM. Those hours were clearly the majority preference.

I looked at my secretary appalled, and then laughed. 'Take these ballots to the shredder and be on notice. Your lips are sealed!"

Career Snapshot: Introduction to Cuba

I can't speak for those whose career has taken them to Mongolia, or Zaire, or countless other posts far from Toledo, Ohio, but I would challenge anyone to identify an assignment where the challenges and rewards are as striking as those offered by Cuba. Fidel Castro has outlasted, some would say out maneuvered nine American presidents. And we expect Our Man in Havana to deal successfully with Fidel. And while doing so, we also expect him to not run afoul of the highly charged and very politically successful Cuban exile community in Miami. Those are the challenges, and they are fairly self-evident if nearly unique. In contrast, after forty some years of Fidel, the rewards of a Cuban assignment have been largely forgotten, but they are still there. Cuba is truly the Pearl of the Antilles. Although we were in Cuba from the early to mid 1980s when the Cold War was still very alive and thus those challenges were very clear before our eyes, we also enjoyed the Cubans and their country as we have enjoyed few other posts.

Chapter Nine

I never refuse. I never contradict. I sometimes forget.

Benjamin Disraeli

When dealing with adversaries, diplomats from superpower America play the game with a strong hand. Even when we speak softly, as Teddy Roosevelt advised, our adversaries know we carry a big stick and incorporate that fact in their own policy. They may not truckle to us when we make policy demands upon them that they would prefer to avoid, but they don't often confront us with a challenge that might provoke a serious economic, political, or military response. Rather, they dig into a bag of diplomatic gambits that may include delay, obfuscation, spurious counter proposals, and other non-replies. Almost all Foreign Service Officers have during the course of their careers made hard hitting demarches only to see their counterpart bob and weave in this manner. But I wonder how many were stymied by chutzpah, which is pure "unmitigated effrontery?" I've had that experience, but only in Cuba. That may suggest something about the durability of the Castro regime but I'll let readers draw that judgment.

This is a tale of two cities, Mexico City and Havana. Two cities that in very different ways have given ulcers to U.S. policymakers and diplomats for over a hundred years. The tale is also based on two nasty features of contemporary international relations—insurgencies and narcotics—that drive traditional diplomats into early retirement.

I had been deputy chief of mission in Mexico during the period when the narcotics cartels in Colombia were hitting their stride and Castro's Cuba was simultaneously supporting insurgences in Central America and Soviet-leaning governments in Africa that were fighting anti-communist insurgences. We at the time were coping ineffectually with exploding demand for narcotics at home and were supporting governments in Central America and insurgents in Africa.

Had I been serving in the same position in, say Buenos Aires or Bonn, I doubt that this mix of headaches and ulcers would have occupied much of my day-to-day work. But I was in Mexico City.

Colombian narcotraffickers were beginning in those years to use Mexico as a transshipment route. The Mexican government didn't like that one bit and, to the best of its ability, cooperated with us in trying to cut off the transshipments. Washington liked that but was far from pleased with Mexico's lack of cooperation in stopping the insurgents in Central America. Worse, the Mexican government, or at least the Mexican foreign ministry, actually seemed to like Fidel and the Central American insurgents.

The reaction of the Department to this mishmash of problems and players was to send me instructions to bang on Mexican desks. Although they were all too polite to say so, I'm sure that the senior officials in the foreign ministry and the ministry of government were growing mighty bored with me.

But the worst was yet to come, both from their perspective and mine. Shortly before Christmas in the early 1980s, a notorious Colombian narcotrafficker—call him Jaime—was observed by the Mexican narcotics police, who had him under surveillance, to visit both the Cuban and Nicaraguan embassies, the latter then under Sandinista management. His visits seriously puzzled the narcotics police, because narcotics traffickers at that time were known for their free enterprise rather than collectivist orientation. And more to the point, the narcotics police had no intelligence indicating that these two embassies were in any way involved in the drug trade. But Jaime was a bad one, and he was not known to act capriciously. So the narcotics police advised the Mexican national security police, and the latter threw him in jail. I'm not sure of the grounds on which they charged him, but Mexican prosecutors always acted as if they had a lot of discretionary authority.

Both Mexican police forces told their embassy counterparts—the DEA and the FBI—of Jaime's arrest and they in turn cabled their U.S. headquarters. Although I had seen those reporting cables, it was the response that involved me. And it came from State. There were multiple arrest warrants against Jaime in the U.S., and the DEA and the FBI wanted us to extradite him. So State instructed me to begin the proceedings. However, State also said that the Colombian government had arrest warrants for Jaime and suggested that I work with the Colombian embassy. The Colombians wanted him not only for narcotics trafficking but also for gun running. Apparently the thought of those planes returning empty after dropping off cocaine in the Bahamas was too much for Jaime's business sensibility. And that led him to begin supplying arms to the Colombian guerrillas.

So I met with the Colombian ambassador, and we began to plan our strategy. It was going to be tricky. The Mexican foreign office then didn't like to turn anyone over to the Gringos, regardless of his criminal record. On the face of it a Colombian request for extradition would seem to be more likely to produce results. And in fact, from a legal standpoint it was also the stronger of the two cases. But narcotraffickers had found Colombian jails to be quite porous, and we both wanted Jaime put away for a long time. So we recommended to our principals that the U.S. request be given precedence and that we hold the Colombian request as a fallback position.

The Office of the Legal Adviser in State agreed and began working up the formal request for extradition. In the meantime the Colombian ambassador and I began to make the rounds of the foreign ministry, the ministry of government (responsible for the police), and the attorney general. Our ambassador and I even called on the Mexican president. Our messages were all the same: "We want Jaime." If there really is such a thing as diplomatic pressure we were bringing it to bear.

The Mexican president told our ambassador and me that we should tell Washington that we definitely would get Jaime. The minister of government and the attorney general were equally forthcoming. Even the deputy foreign minister said the right things, although in looking back I see that he gave himself a few outs.

The problems began when I finally submitted our extradition request to the foreign ministry. That didn't happen overnight. By now it was probably May. After submitting the request, I began calling the foreign ministry's legal adviser every day or so. Sometimes he'd promise me prompt action. Sometimes he asked for clarification of minor points. Sometimes he was out and never found time to return my call. In brief, I was getting the runaround.

But we couldn't go back to the president at that point. There was no real proof of a runaround, even though it was evident. So I went back to the minister of government. He, after all, was actually holding Jaime. It was at this time that the tale takes on the flavor of international spice. "John," the minister confided, leaning over to emphasize the point by touching my knee, "You've got to start pushing much harder. Your Cuban colleague is weighing in with the foreign minister."

I immediately checked with friends in the foreign ministry and, sure enough, the Cuban ambassador was urging the foreign minister to reject the extradition request and release Jaime. But I couldn't learn why the Cuban was seeking Jaime's release. Washington loved my report of that conversation!

Almost immediately I got instructions to insist that the Mexicans honor our extradition request—what did they think I had been doing for the past five months?—and so I made the rounds still again, and again. And I was still making them in June when I was unexpectedly transferred—to Havana! I was to be head of the U.S. Interests Section, our ambassador without title, Our Man in Havana.

* * *

While on home leave I received a letter from a friend in the embassy telling me that the Mexicans, without advance warning, had put Jaime on a plane to Madrid, and that we had subsequently lost sight of him. The Cuban ambassador had won. Or perhaps I should say that the Mexican foreign office had chalked up a few more points in its never-ending struggle to right the wrongs of 1847. So much for the Mexican president's assurances. I had understood when he had to renege on the Shah, but this broken promise teed me off.

* * *

I had been in Havana for about six months when Jaime entered my life again. Not that he was now in Havana, at least to my knowledge. I brought him onto the scene in order to counter a particularly hypocritical maneuver by Castro. This was the first time that Castro contacted me in order to communicate with the U.S. Administration.

Castro wanted, and probably still wants, effective communication with the U.S. Administration. Since the

Department turns its shoulder on the Chief of the Cuban Interests Section in Washington, Castro knows he has to go through the resident Yankee. In order to do so he designates three or four of his top foreign policy advisors to be points of contact with the Chief of the U.S. Interests Section. Through these men, and they were all men, I was probably in closer contact with Castro than were any of my full-fledged ambassadorial colleagues.

On this occasion, I was called by the secretary of my chief contact. She asked if he could come by my residence immediately to discuss something of the "highest urgency." Of course I said, "Of course. I'll meet him in thirty minutes."

I was intrigued. He could have come to the office. By suggesting the residence, he seemed to be underscoring the importance of what he wanted to tell me. But then again, maybe he just wanted some good scotch and a cigar. This contact, by the way, was a personal friend of Fidel as well as a high official in the secret police. For cover, he was also the head of tourism, not that there was much tourism in Cuba at that time. So I was definitely intrigued. The possible subject matter that this guy might raise was wide-ranging indeed.

It was only a minute or so after I arrived at the residence that he was at the door. He must have been waiting around the corner. Ushering him into the library, I offered him a scotch and a cigar. He declined. My antennae now were definitely quivering, but I did ask the maid to bring coffee.

Fidel's friend got right to the point. "John, I'm sure that you have been informed about the indictments brought, in absentia, by the U. S. District Attorney in Florida against two of our serving general officers." If this were chess, I'd have thought that here was an opening move for which I was truly unprepared, since all I knew was what I had read in the Miami Herald. So I decided to counter with the Cavour gambit. "Well, actually, all I know is what I've read in the Miami Herald. Aren't they being charged with facilitating the efforts of Colombian narcotics traffickers by allowing them to use Cuban airfields and coastal waters? And, of course, I've read your government's rebuttal in Granma.[1] But that is about it."

It may seem strange, but Washington hadn't told me anything about the indictments. And even during those few months that I had been in Cuba I had gotten so used to charges, denials, and counter-charges that officials of both governments hurled at each other through the press that I usually read and forgot them. Especially when I had no official role in the matter, as in this case.

Fidel's friend looked at me for a while, judging, I suppose, whether I knew more than I had admitted. Then he continued: "The Comandante en Jefe has asked me to give you a message about this slanderous matter that he would like you to send to the President."

I was immediately both on guard and amused. On guard because my contact, like almost every other Cuban, usually

---

[1] Granma is the official newspaper of the Cuban Communist Party. It is named after the yacht Castro bought from an American and used to ferry his first guerrillas to Cuba. The American had named the yacht after, you guessed it, his grandmother. A nice historical irony.

referred to Castro as "Fidel." Calling him commander-in-chief signaled something big. But I was also amused, because I couldn't help wondering how many desks a message from me would pass over before it reached the President, if ever. I also questioned why Castro wanted to communicate with the President. A diplomatic note would have done the job just as well. Later during my years in Havana I developed an answer to that question, but that is another tale.

Fidel's friend shifted his vocal cords down to an appropriately weighty tone, looked me in the eye, and declared, "The Comandante en Jefe would like you to tell the President that we are revolutionaries. For revolutionaries, trafficking in narcotics is against all of our principles."

The message continued along these lofty themes for several minutes. While my contact droned on, my thoughts were drawn to Mexico, Jaime, and my defeat by the Cuban ambassador. It was probably at this point that I began to think about how a small country might play a poor hand with chutzpah, although I wasn't yet ready to put that name on it. Less than a year after springing a truly big-league trafficker from a Mexican jail, and Castro is pouting about his revolutionary innocence and purity!

After my contact finally concluded Castro's message, I allowed a longish pause to set the stage, while I tried to look as if I were pondering the awesome weight of the message. I then said, "I don't know much about revolutionary purity, and as I said, I don't know more about the facts of the Florida indictments than what I have read in the papers.

Therefore, I can't speak to whether or not the U.S. Government is making a 'grave error.' But [another pause] I do have personal knowledge of a case involving Cuban officials and a notorious narcotics trafficker. And that case seems to raise more questions, at least to me, than Fidel's message answers."

I then recounted in numbing detail the odyssey of Jaime from his visits to the Nicaraguan and Cuban embassies in Mexico City to his disappearance in Madrid. Throughout my tale, Fidel's friend betrayed not the slightest twitch of surprise or discomfort. He listened to me as passively as I had listened to him. And when I had finished, he too paused.

And then he picked up his coffee, leaned back in his chair, crossed his legs, and calmly explained, "We never said that Jaime wasn't a friend. But we only deal with him when he is wearing his gun runner hat and not when he wears his narcotics hat."

That is when the thought about the uses of chutzpah truly came into focus. I immediately understood that my contact had effectively sidestepped my rejoinder. What could I possibly say to him? "Friend, you are displaying unmitigated effrontery?" No, he had used chutzpah to play that hand to a draw, and so I let the cards lie there between us.

Career Snapshot: Dollar Diplomacy

Cuba in the early 1980s: hours-long diatribes against the "new nazi fascist barbarians" (that's us), troops in Angola doing their "fraternal internationalist duty," Committees for the Defense of the Revolution marching in support of the Sandinistas, billboards everywhere depicting the martyred Ché Guevara: the "Heroic Guerrilla." It was Revolution writ large. Well, not quite.

"John, I know we have got to take the Stosses and the Rawns. I know that they'll love it. But quite frankly, I'm getting tired of long-legged mulattas."

"Speak for yourself, Sue. Cuban culture is not to be sneered at."

Castro waged a revolution not only against a dictatorship, but against the decadence allowed, even fostered, by the dictatorship. Batista and the Mob, Batista and gambling, Batista and prostitution. Comes the revolution it will all be different. And it was, and the tourist dollars dried up.

A decade-long pause to think about it.

And then, "hey, maybe it wasn't all that bad. Now the Tropicana, that was Cuban culture, that wasn't decadent."

So the daughters of those long-legged mulattas of the '50s got out their mamas' fishnet hose, bongo drummers flexed their fingers, and trumpeters and trombonists listened to old Tito Puentes recordings to recapture that certain frenzy. Then they wheeled out those sexually suggestive statues that used to grace the entry way, dusted the tables and greased the elevator stage, and the Tropicana was again ready for business. All this was about five or so years before we arrived. They had it down pat by the time we first saw the show.

Picture an outdoor nightclub. The Southern Cross overhead. Royal palms and bougainvillea for walls. A seashell bandstand. Trumpets blare. Trombones moan. Bongos go wild. The elevator stage rises. And from stage right and left those long, fish-netted legs rumba out. You're sitting right next to the stage. Waiters heap your table with large dishes of wonderful, greasy pork. Bottles of rum are replaced at the first hint that you might be reaching the bottom.

No wonder they brought it back. You'd have to be insane to make a revolution against this.

We took every guest who visited us, sometimes several times. They all loved it—well, the men certainly did. They'd watch those long legs swirl through the opening number. They'd finally look up at the great bodies above the legs and at those wonderful smiles above the bodies. And then when the mistress of ceremonies strode onto the stage they'd ask me to translate. She too was striking, if a bit older, probably a graduate of that rumba line. She'd welcome the audience to the show and then announce proudly that there were some very special guests present: "Please welcome the Bulgarian Young Communists!"

Loud cheers came from way behind the royal palms. Your guests peered into the dark trying to see the prominentes.

"Please welcome a delegation of Soviet coal miners. Their visit is in recognition of exceptional work."

More cheers from even further back. And so it went.

Then our guests would blurt out, "But how does the representative of the 'new nazi fascist barbarian' get a stage side table with all the pork we can eat and all the rum we can drink while the communist soul mates are in the parking lot?"

And my reply was so satisfying: "It's very simple. When making the reservations, my secretary always says that we will pay in U. S. dollars!"

Chapter Ten

I am making great progress in the art of saying nothing in a great many words.

Otto von Bismarck

Our stay in Havana offered friends a unique opportunity to visit Cuba and get a first hand view of Castro's Revolution. American citizens can spend U.S. dollars in Cuba only if they first obtain a license from our Treasury Department. That is not easy since Treasury does not give such licenses for purposes of tourism. And if you can't spend dollars it is pretty hard to visit Cuba. For their part the Cuba authorities have a pretty limiting visa policy. So not many Americans have visited Cuba in the past forty years. But as a courtesy, Treasury and the Cuban authorities would give licenses and visas to our friends. Many took advantage of that courtesy.

Generally while serving as tour guides we'd try to limit our comments to factual explanations. Let the guests draw their own conclusions about Castro Cuba's strange ways before talking about them. When we did talk later in the residence, around the pool or over drinks Sue or I would often observe that what our guests had just seen was quite different from what they would see in the "Real Latin America." That phrase *raised* more questions than it answered, however. Our guests would express doubts that anything "real" that was the product of 500 years of cultural development could be erased in mere decades. They'd then ask if we hadn't seen real Latin American traits pushing through the veneer of Castro's new socialist society. Those were good questions and they caused us to be more careful observers.

Cuba up till then was our only experience with daily life in a communist society, and I think that is why we saw the contrasts rather than the similarities with our previous Latin American experience. Take a few examples that may not strike you as strange but that astounded us:

Everyone arrives at work and social events on time.

The few who are fortunate enough to have a car obey traffic lights and don't blow their horns.

In markets, at bus stops, before ticket booths, everyone waits in orderly lines and no one pushes ahead.

These were Cubans! It was crazy. And then there were the physical aspects of the new socialist world. Where the citizenry had to interact with officialdom, such as with migration officials at the airport, in police stations, or in a government office that controlled any form of private activity, the officials sat in booths whose counter was at eye level. You could only interact with that official from the posture of a supplicant looking up to the dispenser of goodies.

Sue coined a phrase for these so un-Latin features of Fidel's Cuba: DictoKit. She meant that when Fidel declared himself to be a communist and turned to the Soviets for support, he didn't limit his shopping to guns and trade credits. He also sought out all of those other devices and procedures in a communist dictatorship's kit bag of controls that enables it to force its citizens to act as if they were in straitjackets.

I could see why Fidel adopted the DictoKit. It worked. What puzzled me when we first saw the DictoKit being used is that I didn't hear any average Cuban complaining. And then there were those gatherings of the masses in the Plaza of the Revolution where tens of thousands of Cubans cheered Fidel as he spoke interminably about everything under the sun. They actually seemed to like it.

The first concrete hint that we had indeed been missing Cuba's underlying Latin American roots—that revolutionary fervor was not shared by everyone—came during our second July 26th celebration. Fidel began his revolution on that date with an attack on an army barracks in Santiago de Cuba. It is now the Cuban national day, and he celebrates it with a major speech in a different city each year. That year was the 25th anniversary, so of course the celebration had to be in Santiago. And he made sure that the entire diplomatic corps would be in attendance.

The corps was flown to Santiago in the afternoon before the big day. It was our first visit to Santiago, so Sue and I broke away from the arrival party laid on for the dips and walked around the town. We were both enthralled with Santiago. None of the buildings appeared to be recently constructed; in fact, to our eyes it seemed that there had been little physical change since Fidel's revolution, so most of the colonial and 19th- and early 20th-century buildings were intact. Also intact were the royal palms, flame trees, and jacarandas that lined most of the streets. Santiago was a jewel of a Caribbean time capsule. Sue looked at it all with wonder and opined that if we could buy some of those old homes we would make a bundle when Castro finally went. My ever-practical bride.

As we ambled along I noticed that every home had what appeared to be a three-by-five-inch postcard tacked to the door. Intrigued, I told Sue to keep watch while I scurried up to the nearest porch to read one of the cards. Before she could protest that that might not be a good idea, I was on the porch. The card was a printed form to be filled in by recipients. It read:

> This dwelling will send 6 occupants to the Plaza of the Revolution July 26 to celebrate with Fidel.
>
> José Mendez head of household
>
> Julia Salsimendi Block Chairman, Committee for the Defense of the Revolution

A chapter was added to our book on the DictoKit. I was willing to bet a bundle that Julia Salsimendi would play a big role in tomorrow's festivities.

And so it turned out. We were sitting on our hotel balcony waiting for the diplocade to take us to the Plaza where Fidel would speak. Ordinary Cubans filled the street, streaming by. They were clearly marching in groups of twenty or so, and at the head of each group was a woman holding high an umbrella.

"Will you look at that? The block chairman defending the Revolution by herding her charges along. If we hadn't seen those postcards, you might think that she was just a cheery if officious tour guide. But she's really the Cuban Madam LaFarge."

Sue laughed politely. She's not overly enthralled with my literary linkages.

But then it got even better. At the Plaza the diplomatic wives had choice seats front and center, while the chiefs of mission actually sat on the stage with Fidel. That sounds impressive, but we actually could see little but the audience. So Sue had to tell me about this next scene.

When the block chairmen had seated their wards and made sure that none could sneak out, a door in the front of the podium upon which Fidel would speak opened. Inside the little room formed by the podium, Sue could see the upper torso of a man. She said that this guy started pointing to the different sections of the Plaza. Looking around, she saw that in each section other men rose to acknowledge the cue. Then when Fidel began to speak, the upper torso inside the podium would make a variety of hand signals and, on those cues, his cohorts would lead the audience in cheers, laughter, or what have you. He was the official cheerleader, a prompter at the edge of the stage but prompting the audience rather than the actor.

There could be no doubt, in the New Socialist Cuba revolutionary fervor was too important to be left in the hands of the masses. It was then that we began to modify some of our initial impressions. If the masses had to be corralled into serving as the scene-setting cast of thousands, it probably was because as Latin American individualists most of them otherwise would have stayed away. But that conclusion held for the masses. What about the party apparatchiks, those who staff out the New Socialist Cuba? The answer to that question came some months later, also during a ceremony honoring the 25th anniversary of the Revolution.

This tale also puts flesh on the bones of all those old jokes about the similarities between Karl and Groucho Marx. By way of background, to explain why I was where I was when the faithful let their fervor down, perhaps the most irritating aspect of the Cuban assignment was the requirement that all of my contact with Cubans, private and public, had to be arranged through the Ministry of Foreign Relations. With direct contact thus limited, my analysis of what Fidel was up to had to be based on secondary sources. I learned to read the party press for what was not said. I read Fidel's speeches for foreign-policy thoughts that might escape during a three-hour discourse on Cuban dairy farms. And I went to every event to which I was invited.

I had just gone through the morning mail and found an invitation for that evening to an event commemorating the 25th anniversary of the founding of the Ministry of Foreign Relations—MinRex, to use the Cuban acronym. (The Cuban official calendar begins with the Triumph of the Revolution in 1959. All previous developments are non-events. It was if there had been no Ministry of Foreign Relations before the Revolution.) So I picked up the phone, called Sue and told her were going to the Karl Marx Theater to hear the vice president, Carlos Rafael Rodríguez, speak about the glories of Cuban diplomacy. She hung up on me without replying, but I knew she'd go. Sue was a professional, but even professionals don't always have to like what they have to do for their country.

That evening we arrived at the Karl Marx Theater well before the appointed hour, aware that the New Socialist Man was punctual. The elite of Cuba streamed up in their Soviet-built 1960s-style Fiats, called Ladas. My diplomatic colleagues arrived in their Mercedeses. I drove a Ford, which says something about the Foreign Service, but I'm not sure what. In automobile-starved Cuba, the swirling of so much horsepower knocking loudly on very low-octane gasoline was a sure sign that this was a must-attend event. We entered and took seats reserved for "dips." After settling in and looking around, Sue whispered, "Listen to how little chatter there is beyond the seats reserved for diplomats. I suspect that this crew knows what's coming and that it's not going to be pretty."

She then leaned forward to talk to the French ambassador, leaving me to my own thoughts. We really were in a theater.

The curtains were closed. I wondered if they planned to begin with a film. I was wrong again.

However, when the drama began, it was appropriately theatrical. Trumpets blared, and then blared again. When the music shifted to a military march, two color guards from the Revolutionary Armed Forces goose-stepped down the two aisles, mounted the stage, and stood at attention stage left and stage right. The curtains parted, revealing three banks of desks behind which were standing, and applauding, officials of MinRex and other government luminaries. They were perched behind the lectern like monkeys in a tree.

The guards planted the flags. A young woman strode determinedly to the lectern and read the Pledge of the Revolution. This exercise requires the reader to reel off the tasks still ahead of the successful Cuban revolutionaries (such as, at that time, humping a pack and an AK-47 through the jungles of Angola). After each exciting task, the audience of excited revolutionaries shouts, "Comandante en Jefe, Mándeme," which roughly translates, "Fidel, just tell me what to do." Sue leaned toward me and whispered, "They think that is how to warm up an audience: Hi Ho, Hi Ho, with Fidel to War We Go ?" I merely grunted a reply; I sensed she was not going to be on her diplomatic best behavior that evening.

When this litany was completed, the foreign minister rose to introduce the vice president. Speaking for about 30 minutes, the minister worked on the principle that gross flattery is always acceptable. Sue nudged me again. "Look at the top row, right side." There, a non-voting member of the Central Committee had drifted into sleep.

His head had fallen back and his mouth was opening.

Bolstered with the laudatory introduction, the vice president rose beaming and strode to the lectern, where he announced that his subject for the evening was the history of MinRex. While I can't honestly say that I heard an audience-wide moan, I did see mournful looks exchanged that suggested many understood what lay ahead, that the vice president planned to discuss the *entire* history of MinRex. Which he proceeded to do. The organization of his presentation was calendric. You start with day one and move forward. He spoke for two hours and 54 minutes. I timed him.

At first I conscientiously tried to follow his remarks. You never know where and when you'll find the key piece of the analytical puzzle that you are working on. But only the demented or the saintly could have succeeded in that task. I was neither, but neither was anyone else among the hundreds who had met their obligation and crowded into Karl Marx's revenge.

Quite soon the non-voting member of the Central Committee was snoring, rather loudly. About 25 minutes into the discourse, a full-voting member rose, caught the eyes of several of his colleagues, bent a bit at the waist and grimaced slightly, thereby conveying to them, and to the entire audience whom he faced, that his bladder was bursting. He exited stage left, never to return. By an hour into the history lesson, three more panel members had dozed off.

But the juices were flowing in the veins of at least some of those on stage. Her face bright red from swallowing laughter, Sue pounded my ribs and choked out, "Stage right, second row!" There, a MinRex official and a woman from the Ministry of Foreign Commerce whom I had seen before had sunk into their seats and were almost hidden from audience view. Almost, but not quite. In the vernacular of my high school and college days, they were making out like mad.

Meanwhile, in the audience a game of bridge was underway among my more experienced and foresighted diplomatic colleagues; more and more Cubans were copping the bladder plea; and chatter ebbed and flowed but soon settled into a constant background theme contrapuntal to the lyrics of the history lesson.

The vice president reached the mid 1970s toward the close of the second hour and promised that he would treat the more recent past in greater detail than he had sketched the 1960s and early 1970s. I am certain that at this point I did hear a moan from the audience. They knew that he would be true to his word.

This grueling evening occurred in 1984. When the vice president passed through 1983—one year to go—the panel and the audience alike perked up and began to eye the exits. They knew that they weren't home free yet, but the end was in sight. Then the vice president made an error equivalent to that made by the quartermaster of the British Army in the Crimea, when, after delivering supplies to the colonel of the Light Brigade, yelled back to him across the battlefield, "You want to charge that?" And off rode the 600. So with the vice president when, with almost a full year of history still to be related, he began the annals of 1984 with, "And so in conclusion..."

The experienced panel and audience, aware that there wouldn't be a second chance, jumped to their feet and began applauding wildly. The vice president continued to speak, but the applause rolled over him. He struggled up verbally again, only to be drowned by the next breaking wave of cheering. Then the color guard gave the coup de grace. With trumpets blaring, they-goose stepped back up the aisles to the stage and recaptured their flags. It was the signal. The panelists raced each other for the exits, both stage right and left. The audience ran for the doors, most beating the color guards. The vice president and foreign minister were left alone on the stage staring morosely at each other. Sue was slumped in her seat, tears of laughter streaming down her face.

That evening, in retrospect, was good for my soul. I found that even Cuban apparatchiks have a bit of the real Latin in them. If nothing else, I couldn't imagine Soviet apparatchiks making out on stage.

Career Snapshot: Crisis Management

"Sir, these five info copies came in just as I was about to dismantle the system. They are all Secret and the subject is Grenada."

"Shred them and continue shutting down!"

I had just returned to the chancellery after delivering a diplomatic note to the Cuban foreign minister. Cuban and U.S. troops were shooting at each other in Grenada. Our military operation had begun early that morning. The Assistant Secretary had called me before dawn, telling me that the invasion was underway and dictating the note that I was to translate and deliver immediately. That note was right out of the 19th century: Cuba is not the objective of our intervention; order your construction brigade to lay down its arms and it can depart Grenada with honor and flags flying.

Nice words, but the thought that gripped me was from the late 20th century: Teheran and the hostage crisis! My staff and I were truly isolated. If the fact that Cuban and American troops were shooting it out on Grenada pushed Fidel to retaliate, we in the Interests Section were the logical target, or so I thought. And Washington couldn't evacuate us short of an invasion. So after delivering that note, I called the American staff together and gave instructions to shred the files and prepare to destroy the code machines. Take time to read what the Department was telling other posts about our intervention? Forget it!

Well, I was wrong, of course, but I wasn't the only one in Cuba who got it wrong. That morning I called on my principal channel to Castro in order to reemphasize the message. Our conversation too was pure 19th century. It appeared that he also had read Bismarck's admonition that "Even in a declaration of war, one observes the rules of politeness." I suggested that he phone Castro then and there and ask if Castro wanted me to pass any message back to Washington. My contact readily agreed and went into an adjoining room to make the call. While I only could hear what he said to Castro, I couldn't miss the volume of emotion that the call provoked. My contact returned, obviously shaken. 'The Comandante said, 'Tell Ferch his information has been overtaken. The Cuban troops have fought to the last man defending the flag. Just ask him to find out when the Yankee invaders will send the bodies back.'"

There was not much to say in response to that, so I returned to the chancellery and reported the conversation. Only to be told that it was Castro who was misinformed. The Cuban troops had surrendered and their commander had fled to the Soviet embassy. In Havana the mood was grim, both Castro's and mine.

The killing was over, but the crisis, as seen from my perspective, dragged on for a week. I couldn't assume that Castro wouldn't try to regain the initiative by turning loose the Committees for the Defense of the Revolution on the Interests Section. So I met with the Marine Security Guards to prepare for the worst and with the staff families to try to keep up morale. And while I juggled those balls, Washington inundated me with instructions to try to get the Cubans to wind up the crisis.

Once the shooting was over, Washington wanted to send the Cuban military engineers home and get on with the task of putting Grenada back on its feet, on our side of the fence. But Castro didn't know if he wanted them back quite yet. They were alive after all and not in body bags. So I became a courier again. For whatever reason, all of the incoming messages seemed to arrive between 2:00 and 3:00 AM. The Vice Foreign Minister took to sleeping at the Ministry to await my call. I told my chauffeur that there was no sense in both of us losing sleep every night and that I'd drive myself in.

"There is another one coming in, sir. Top Secret and priority."

So I pulled on pants and a shirt, ran downstairs to the car, raced over to the avenue, and sped into the dark. There was no one else on the roads. But then two pinpricks of brightness reflecting in the rear view mirror caught my eye. They grew larger, soon they were the size of quarters, and then the mirror was like a spotlight. I couldn't help wondering, "Is this when Castro begins to strike back?" But then I saw a Soviet Fiat pulling abreast. Two obvious Cuban secret service types were in the front seat. They looked at me and I swear that I could see them sigh with relief. They must have been asleep when I roared out of the yard. Awakening to find me gone, they must have seen service in Angola on the horizon. Now they could relax.

But not everyone could. Castro did indeed strike back. But not at us. When the boys finally did come home it was to a court martial for the officers. And their commander should have stayed in the Soviet embassy, for Castro did send him to Angola—as a private.

In retrospect I see that the crisis was not in Havana, it was confined to Grenada. Castro was not about to give the Yankees any excuse to turn those troops in Grenada against Cuba. But try telling that to Our Man in Havana at the time. He was too busy trying to keep his staff working on preparations for Teheran II. Burn before reading.

Chapter Eleven

A diplomat is a person who can tell you to go to hell in such a way that you actually look forward to the trip.

Caskie Stinnett

If you read many diplomatic memoirs you might conclude that diplomacy is not dissimilar to a verbal tennis match: "I said to him..." "He countered by saying..." "We proposed five policy options..." For years, I too had lived for the verbal sally and counted metaphoric coup. But one of my most satisfying coups was non-verbal and to add spice to the tale was scored against that master wordsmith—Fidel Castro.

We had driven away from the residence on one of those perfect Caribbean days that Hemingway loved to write about. Clouds sailed like the Great White Fleet along a horizon balanced between lapis lazuli sky and the Prussian blue of the Gulf Stream. Royal palms stretched down the median of the boulevard as far as I could see. Bougainvillea tumbled out of the gardens of the crumbling former mansions of the rich who had fled to rebuild their fortunes in Miami.

It was August, 1982. We had arrived the day before in Havana to take up my duties as Chief of the U.S. Interests Section, our embassy by another name. It was my first full-fledged diplomatic mission. In the absence of formal diplomatic relations I couldn't use the title of ambassador, but that formality was more than offset by the opportunity to match wits with the nemesis of nine American presidents. My deputy, Charlie, had come for breakfast and was driving me to the chancellery.

My adrenalin was pumping. I could see why Hemingway loved this place. Even in its decrepitude, it left other Caribbean cities that I had visited far behind, except perhaps for Cartagena, and the weather seemed better here.

I asked Charlie how long until we reached the chancellery. He pointed to a bridge ahead and explained that we would swing over that and onto the malecón, the road that runs along the sea wall west from the harbor. The chancellery stands about a mile from the harbor and the Moro Castle. Observing that "communist cars" apparently is an oxymoron, and that consequently there isn't any rush-hour jam, Charlie said that that we would be there in several minutes.

Ahead the malecón bulged slightly into the Gulf Stream and a seven-story glass-walled slab filled the bulge. A tropical Bauhaus.

"There she is, John, all yours. Well at least for the next couple of years and provided that you don't screw up.

About the only thing that the Cuban politicos in Havana and Miami have in common is an eagerness to stick a career-ending stiletto in the back of Our Man in Havana. Kind of a common punctuation point to their separate political agendas."

"Charlie, I can see that you are going to be a wonderfully supportive deputy."

At that moment the driver pulled around the slab and I saw my future staring at me. Less than 100 feet from the front entrance of the chancellery and facing it squarely was a very large billboard. It was about 40 to 50 feet long and maybe 20 feet high. It stood in a small park originally intended as a monument to the sailors who lost their lives on the battleship Maine. By its size and also by its message, the billboard completely overshadowed that commemoration of the United States' first intervention in Cuba.

On the billboard was a caricature of Uncle Sam dancing an impotent jig upon the peninsula of Florida. Teeth clenched, he could only utter, "G R R R R R." Across the Gulf Stream, standing proudly on the island of Cuba, a caricature of the simple peasant hero of José Martí's great poem, Guantanamera, held a Russian AK-47 assault rifle above his head and declared, "Mr. Imperialist, we have absolutely no fear!"

As I stared, Charlie explained that Castro had put up the billboard when the Department reopened the chancellery five years before and that he changes the message when each new chief of mission arrives. I had been bade welcome.

I think I laughed and said something about the billboard giving new meaning to the phrase "diplomatic communiqué."

At that moment, my welcoming billboard struck me as humorous. But soon I found that a 50-by-20-foot message can get under your skin. It peers over your cup of coffee in the morning when you are trying to read Fidel's latest four-and-a-half-hour diatribe. It leers at you when you are trying to hold a staff meeting. It chuckles behind your back when the Soviet ambassador pays a courtesy call. It snickers "Good night" when you leave the chancellery in the evening.

Perhaps worse, I seemed to hear that AK-47 waving peasant whenever I met to conduct business with those senior Cuban officials whom Fidel had designated to be my interlocutors. It was as if he were a one-man Greek chorus laughing at the futility of my efforts.

Orders for our Man In Havana: The Sandinistas in Nicaragua have consolidated power but are under pressure from the Contras. There are rumors that the Sandinistas would like to get a couple of MIGs, just in case. So we are taking the initiative. Make a démarche and warn the Cubans not to help the Sandinistas to fly the friendly skies of Central America.

"Mr. Minister, I have been instructed by the highest authorities to tell you that if MIGs are provided the Government of Nicaragua, the United States will take appropriate measures. We will view the provision of MIGs as highly provocative."

"Why are you telling this to me? Washington should be talking to the Nicaraguan Government."

"Mr. Imperialist, we have absolutely no interest in what Washington thinks or what appropriate measures it might take. Stick it in your ear, Mr. Imperialist."

Orders for our Man in Havana: Washington believes that the Cubans are working with Colombian narcotics traffickers, allowing them to take advantage of Cuban bays and cays to run the white powder past our Coast Guard. Make a back-channel approach and warn them that they are playing with fire.

"Martinez, I've been instructed to request that you pass along to the Comandante that we know someone here is helping narcotraficantes slip by our patrols. Can't tell you the source of the information, of course, but we have full faith in its reliability. If this activity continues, it's my judgment that there will be hell to pay and you can kiss goodbye any hope of improving relations."

"Ferch, tell Washington that they are barking up the wrong tree. We are revolutionaries, not narcs. Our hands are clean. No Cuban revolutionary would think to soil them with the white stuff."

"Mr. Imperialist, we are absolutely shocked, shocked that you should think such thoughts of us."

More of the same, week after week, month after month. I bet Kissinger never had to put up with a Greek chorus laughing at his every démarche.

So Fidel knew what he was doing when he had had the billboard erected. It had gotten under my skin and I couldn't get it out of my mind. I had become the playing field of galloping mixed metaphors.

Sue and I were in the living room of the residence having a drink before dinner. I had been brooding, and she asked me if anything was wrong. Normally, this was a moment that could not fail to raise my spirits. We had just had a swim in the residence's Olympic-size swimming pool that sits in seven acres of tropical gardens. The residence itself is an architectural jewel. And early evening in Havana is a delight to all the senses. That evening, however, I was untouched by it all. I stared out at the bronze American eagle mounted at the back of the garden. It had graced the monument to the battleship Maine until some long-forgotten hurricane had toppled it.

The old bird seemed to be scowling directly at me, as if asking when I was going to start earning my paycheck. "It's gotten to me, Sue. I hate to say it, but it's true. That billboard is taking the fun out of diplomacy."

"You mean that you can't concentrate on your golf game, that the snorkeling doesn't bring the old thrill, that the daiquiris leave a sour aftertaste? I understand, your life is really hell. Come off it, John. We'll never have another assignment the likes of this for creature comforts and personal enjoyment. And professionally, you've told me that the Secretary himself has commented favorably on your reporting. What more can you want?"

"I want tit for tat. I want to answer that obnoxious AK 47-waving peasant. I want to send a message to Fidel that will make him growl, ' G R R R R,' impotently. But for the life of me I can't think of a diplomatic way to do it."

"Look, my love, I don't think they mean that billboard to be a personal challenge to you. You seem to get along quite well with the Cubans. They seem to respect you professionally and enjoy your company personally. I think that the billboard is really aimed at the Cuban public. It seems to me that Fidel does not really feel confident that the public is following him enthusiastically in his struggle with the Yankees. The billboard tells them that even though he has to deal with us and allow our presence in Havana, he is not letting down his guard and that they better not either, if they know what's good for them."

"You're right of course. But that's all beside the point. The Cuban people may be the intended audience, not me, but they can't reply to the billboard. Maybe I can. But I don't have a clue as to how."

The months went by. The flamboyants exploded in their blood-orange glory. The frangipanes followed with multi-hued hints of the South Pacific. Our kids came down from college and played Hemingway. The Cold War ground on. The Polish ambassador and I traded bombasts publicly (his side was being nasty to Solidarity at the time) and traded jokes privately. I kept Miami happy with appropriate rhetoric and Washington relatively calm with some rather good analysis of what Fidel was actually up to in Angola. In the fall Sue and I drove the 700 miles to Santiago through rolling seas of sugar cane, by palm-lined beaches designed for travelogues, over the Escambray Mountains and up into the Sierra, where Fidel and his boys had the good fortune to fight the worst army to be cobbled together that century, and down into the colonial jewel of the Caribbean. As Sue suggested, I tried to relax and enjoy it. And succeeded. But I still didn't have any brilliant ideas about a game-winning rejoinder.

That December, without much thought, we decided to give a Christmas party for the chancellery's Cuban staff and for those other Cubans whom Fidel allowed to accept invitations from the Yankees. Those other Cubans were largely from the arts community and, while "safe" from Fidel's perspective, generally either didn't give a damn about politics or understood that it wouldn't be prudent to talk about such subjects. If you could live with that gap in their personalities, they were fine people. We enjoyed them, at any rate, and after many years of immersion in Latin American contemporary and folk art, felt that we could hold our own on their turf. We generally liked the Cuban staff, too. In fact, almost all Cubans are likable. Great dancers. An excitement between the sexes that I had not seen before and haven't seen since. And gluttons for a party.

So we plunged into preparations for the party. Diplomacy can be spelled, "Purveyor of Fine Foods and Beverages." There'd be roast pig, moros y cristianos, and all the other great staples of Cuban cuisine. The bar would never close. There would be dancing inside and out. And in the residence the Christmas tree would look as if we had stolen it from Rockefeller Plaza.

And in fact, it was more than a good party; it was a great party. I rumbaed with a 75-year-old grandmother who put me to shame. Sue led more than 50 Cubans in singing Spanish carols. The food disappeared and the bar stayed open till near dawn. And Cuba's last living world-class artist stood in front of the Christmas tree, sobbing quietly and muttering, "It used to be like this."

We knew that Fidel had banned the celebration of Christmas more than 20 years before but we hadn't guessed how strong the memories were, how deep was the resentment that a Grinch could actually steal Christmas.

After the last guest was rolled out the door, Sue and I, too full of good time to sleep, took a last rum into the garden and told ourselves about the night that we already knew about. The images of mambas and rumbas, carols and roast pig, laughter and tears floated over the garden as if reconvening the party.

Finally, after fully digesting this second time around, Sue said, "I think I see your tit for tat. We'll bring Christmas back to Havana."

In order to fully understand the brilliance of Sue's idea, I have to take you back to the tropical Bauhaus, the American chancellery in Havana. It is seven stories tall. The land on which it sits thrusts gently into the Gulf Stream. The malecón, which has few curves elsewhere, at this point must swerve around our chancellery. Because the chancellery is at right angles to the Stream, drivers and pedestrians on the malecón can see our glass-sided slab for at least a mile in either direction. And the top floor then was truly glass-walled. The roof was held up only by columns at the four comers. In other words, you could look straight through the seventh floor. At one time this glass room had been used as the ambassador's private dining room. The views were spectacular: the Moro Castle, Colonial Havana, 20th-century Havana, the palm- and bougainvillea-shaded suburbs. But we didn't use it for anything. It was empty. Thus Sue's idea.

In that glass box we would erect the biggest Christmas tree we could find in Miami and trim it with as many lights as the aging wiring of the chancellery would permit. We would create a Christmas beacon rivaling the lighthouse on the Moro Castle. Of course we would have to wait, because this holiday season was almost over. But I did not allow the planned Christmas riposte to slip off my agenda.

* * *

Ten months later I called in Sam, the administrative officer, and launched our preparations. I knew that I would have to be somewhat forceful. Sam and my budgetary wish lists did not always overlap.

"Sam, have you got a yellow pad and pencil? No? Well, take these, but don't forget to give them back. I need your help on a project you probably won't like. It's not in the book, I acknowledge, but trust me, I'm confident that it's not against the regs. First, I want you to do a complete measurement of the old ambassadorial dining room, including the exterior measurements of the windows. Yes, I understand that the walls are entirely windows. That's why the top floor has the best view in Havana. Then check the wiring up there. Make sure that it's up to a very heavy load. When you've done that get in touch with someone in Miami who specializes in artificial Christmas trees, lights, and ornaments. No, I don't know how you do that. Call information, ask your mother, write Santa. Tell the guy what the upstairs looks like, give him the dimensions, and ask him for ideas about the largest artificial tree that will fit in the room and the type of colored lights that are really bright. Make sure he understands that I want this to be seen from the Mora Castle to the residence and out into the Gulf Stream as far as the horizon. Ask him also about ornaments that we could hang on the tree that would enhance the brilliance of the lights. Then brief me on what he has to say before we place an order."

Sam was the good soldier. I could almost see his objections begin to form, but he bit them off, shrugged and left my office. (Only to stop and chat with my secretary; so much for urgency.) But some things you can't change, so I swiveled around and looked out the windows, trying to visualize the scene we had planned. And I had to grin because what we planned was only possible because of a loophole in the U.S.-Cuba agreement that authorized the opening of the two interests sections. That agreement forbade any display of national symbols outside the buildings: no flags, no great seals, no name plates, no anything. Although the Cuban Interests Section in Washington was similarly restricted, the restrictions weren't our idea. Castro obviously had wanted to keep the Yankee profile as low as possible. The agreement said nothing about the Cubans erecting a billboard, of course, but it also said nothing at all about what we could do inside the building.

The following week Sam rang me up, said he had the information and the price lists, and asked if he could come up to my office. I said, "sure" and bit my tongue on the question of why a call to Miami had taken a week to make. So in about 15 minutes Sam showed up, sat down and shoved some handwritten notes across the desk. I looked them over quickly. It seemed pretty straightforward. Santa Claus never was a rocket scientist. But before I could say anything, Sam cleared his throat and asked, "Did you take a good look at the bottom line?" "Yeah, why?"

"It's over $3,000, and that's a lot of money to play Santa. And it's going to take a big chunk out of what we planned to do for post morale. You know, the tennis court."

"Sam, you know that I know the budget as well as you do. And so you know that I know that we have put so much fat in there that we ought to put a cholesterol warning on it. And with regard to morale, first, Christmas is a high-morale event and second, I doubt that your tennis game is ever going to improve. So find some other activity to boost your morale, and let me worry about the cost."

"OK, you're the boss, but that means that you can sign the order forms."

I pressed back a smile and nodded agreement thinking that I owed him an explanation. So I pointed out my office window to the billboard and said that I would put money on the table that Fidel's message had rankled every member of the American staff every day they came to work. Asking whether he had ever thought of sending a message back to Castro and waiting for his nod, I expressed my view that the right message had to have double meaning. The Habaneros should welcome it, and it should give Fidel heartburn. "Sam, we're going to return Christmas to Havana and flaunt it in the face of Fidel and his AK-47-waving friend."

When Sam left my office, he was smiling broadly and rushed back to his office, not even stopping to chat with my secretary. Within 20 minutes the order sheet was on my desk for signature.

The chancellery's Ford stake truck needed new shocks. Maneuvering through the potholes on the road to the José Martí International Airport was a sensation not dissimilar to fishing in the chop of the Gulf Stream. Squeezed in the cab with two of our Cuban gofers, I thought that I was about to lose my breakfast several times before we finally reached the customs gate at the airport. Our driver honked the horn to get the domino-playing guards' attention, and one of them ambled over and stuck out his hand. Memories of Mexico flooded back, but Fidel had indeed done away with the mordida, the petty bribery so common elsewhere in Latin America. So I handed over my diplomatic pass, and the guard soon waved us through.

I had insisted on coming along because I didn't want any glitch with Cuban customs that might hold up release of the tree and lights. Since it was par for the course that the support flight was always two hours late, we went into the passenger terminal for coffee. The terminal had a single story and only a few rooms. Fidel had come to power just before the advent of the jet age and the explosion of international travel. Since his domestic and foreign policies tended to dissuade international air travel to Havana, he apparently never felt the need for a modem terminal. With no scheduled flights that day, the place was almost empty. A single elderly male was using an old mop to push a long, dirty rag through figure eights down a terrazzo floor. A few flies lifted off in front of his slow advance. I was reminded of the classic and then contemporary Soviet folk saying: "You pretend to pay me and I pretend to work."

After two hours of sipping the sugary sludge that Cubans in Miami and Havana call coffee, we heard the plane begin its approach. It's really uncanny how our support flights seemed to run on scheduled delays. These flights were a unique feature of our life in Havana. Washington was convinced that its brave diplomats were enduring hardships beyond measure and, to make our life a bit more bearable, chartered bimonthly frights from Miami for mail and any other necessities we might order. Neither my predecessors nor I ever disabused the Department of its conviction.

The Cessna rolled to a stop, and with a Cuban guard riding shotgun, we drove out to meet it. There were no hitches, and after unloading what seemed like a ton of Christmas ornamentalia and passing an hour with Cuban customs paper-pushers, we were on our way back to the chancellery. It was December 4th.

The next day was a Saturday, so I had to authorize overtime for some of the gofers. I had told them to be at the chancellery at 9:00 AM. In the meantime, Sue and I had breakfast.

"Want some more orange juice?" she asked, pushing the pitcher toward me in anticipation of my answer. It was freshly squeezed and nicely chilled. Who could resist? So I poured myself a glass and then gave myself a second helping of mangu, the Caribbean breakfast of champions. You boil some plantains, then mash them with a fork, fry them in oil with chopped onions and peppers, and top the mound off with several fried eggs. Takes three days to digest. I wanted to be up to full strength for the day ahead.

After watching me with gastronomic dismay for some minutes, Sue said that she wanted to get the show on the road, and we went out to the car.

It was another one of those damned perfect Havana days. As I swung onto the malecón, the Great White Fleet of clouds was still proudly sailing the horizon between Prussian blue sea and lapis lazuli sky. Believe me, even with our plan approaching the moment of truth, it was hard to think about Christmas in that setting.

I pulled the car around the chancellery to the entrance, mentally gave my peasant nemesis the finger, and walked up the steps to the front door. The Marine security guard already had it open; he had heard what was planned and wanted to help. Several others of the American staff had also come down to be part of history. If I could have looked into the future and seen George Foreman declaring for Meineke Mufflers, "I'm not going to take it anymore!", I would have said that he described our mood perfectly.

Riding the elevator to the glass-enclosed top floor, I began to worry if Sam had ordered enough lights. I needn't have.

"John, watch where you're stepping." Sam had already unboxed the lights. The strands were everywhere. He stood in the middle of the room as if in a pit of brilliantly colored vipers. I would have preferred that he wait, but what the hell, he had, after all, taken my advice and found something other than tennis to boost his morale. After untangling the vipers, we set to work assembling the tree.

Sue was ecstatic. She told Sam that he had outdone himself. The tree was a beauty.

The bottom branches must have spread over ten feet and the top pushed against the ceiling perhaps twelve feet up. Fidel would be able to see this one even without lights.

Sam was more than pleased with that praise. Beaming, he said that after he had explained our situation to the dealer, the dealer suggested a special order. To me it looked as if that order was patterned on the tree at Rockefeller Center. It was not only big; it had reinforced branches. Sam said that the dealer had guaranteed that the monster would support more than 200 strands of lights. I was delighted.

So we put the dealer to the test and weren't disappointed. The tree took 217 strands. Sue started giving instructions as if, well, she were the Chief of the U.S. Interests Section. "More lights here, more lights there, put the reflectors towards the trunk." The staff didn't bat an eye. They recognized the tone of authority when they heard it.

Sue was deeply into the Christmas spirit. But that is probably poorly phrased. Striving for comeuppance is not usually considered an aspect of the Christmas Spirit.

It was now well past noon and clearly time for lunch, but no one wanted to quit. So we opened some cold beers and began outlining the windows with strands of lights. In fact we double-stranded them. When that was done, we turned the show on to test the wiring, and it held. But of course in the glare of the Caribbean sun we couldn't judge the visual impact of our extravaganza. So we waited.

We had to wait. It was only December 5th. In the "real" Latin America, the Christmas season begins December 8th with the celebration of the Immaculate Conception. We were bringing Christmas back to Havana, and we were going to do it right!

6:00 P.M. December 8th. The sun is setting beyond the suburbs, but full darkness is an hour away. The Marine on duty has instructions to play it safe and not to throw the switch until 7:30. So we are going to have an early dinner. But first, we took some muscle-toning laps and then some anticipatory rum. Excitement runs high. We will not score a complete surprise, since the Cuban staff will have reported to their keepers what we have done. They have no choice. But I doubt that the keepers have any idea of what the show will look like. For that matter, we don't, either.

We're called to dinner. Some fish dish. We'll eat dessert later. It's still twilight, but deepening. What the hell, let's go now.

I speed down the boulevard. Sue is jittery. Over the bridge and I slow down. And there it is.

Christmas at K-Mart! The colors shoot out from all sides of the top floor of the chancellery as if it were a friendly volcano. And at the center of the caldera, clearly visible from at least a mile and a half away, the Christmas tree!

As we slowly passed the chancellery, I noticed that a small group of Habaneros had gathered across the malecón, but thought little of it. Sue wanted to view the show from another angle so we drove down the malecón, crossed the harbor and wound out to the Mora Castle. The show was truly incredible. A multi-colored jewel floated above the dimmed Pearl of the Antilles. Sue took my hand and said, 'Tit for tat!"

The next evening during dinner I received a call from a very agitated Marine. "Sir, there is a large crowd around the building, and two police cruisers just arrived. I don't know what to make of it. I think that you had better get down here."

"Sue, I think our tit for tat is blowing up in our face. I've got to run down to the chancellery and see what the hell is going on!"

So I rushed to the car and, once again, sped down the boulevard, over the bridge and out onto the malecón. I tried to think what the crowd and the police might mean. The only thought I had was not a pleasant one. Fidel was not amused and had called out the Committees for the Defense of the Revolution to protest the Yankee-led return of Christmas to Havana. If so, for once Miami would cheer me, but I doubted that the Secretary would be amused.

As I approached the chancellery I saw that the crowd was indeed a large one, and seemed to be growing. It was gathering from all directions. But it was also moving. Long lines of Habaneros slowly walked around the chancellery and up and down the malecón. There were many family groups. They were obviously looking at the Christmas tree. No one was shouting or yelling and all seemed to be in a jovial mood.

And then I saw the police. They were traffic police. They had been sent by the powers that be—reluctantly, I assume—to keep the crowds moving, but not to make an even bigger scene by trying to chase them away. Four were handling the convening pedestrians and two were in mid-malecón keeping more cars than I knew Havana could boast of moving. And the cops had parked their cruisers in the only spaces available: at either end of my billboard. It was as if the Grinch had sent them to protect his favorite AK-47-waving peasant from the Christmas spirit.

It was a crowning moment. It was a perfect tit for tat. But if I were to express it verbally I would say,

"Yes, Fidel, there is a Christmas."

Chapter Twelve

I asked Tom if countries always apologized when they had done wrong and he says, 'Yes, the little ones does.'

Mark Twain, *Tom Sawyer Abroad*

Castro is truly an exception among Latin American national leaders, and probably among most political leaders elsewhere as well. Obviously, he has been a national leader far longer than any of his peers. More to the point, he is recognizable to many, many people in the Western Hemisphere. Probably the great majority of those people do not think about Castro even several times a year. However, if you were to take a survey and ask, "Who is Fidel Castro?" I'd bet a bundle that most would correctly identify the man. By way of contrast I'd also wager that if other national leaders, the U.S. President excepted, were to be seen walking alone down a side street of their capital, none would be recognized by other than their immediate family and political junkies. And when you start thinking about hemispheric leaders from the past, forget it. Even Perón probably would not be remembered were it not for his wife, Evita. The question is, why is Castro the exception? I started thinking about that question when Castro insisted that I give the President his message about clean hands in the narcotics business.

During the Cold War the answer in part was substantive. Castro, allied with the Soviets, meddled in matters that were truly dangerous and for that reason he was often front-page news. The Cuban Missile Crisis made him internationally notorious, but there were also Cuban military interventions in Zaire, Ethiopia, and Angola in Africa and support for guerrilla insurgencies in Latin America from Bolivia, through the Caribbean to Central America. But the Cold War is long over, and Castro is now reduced to puttering around his own garden. So why are we still aware of him?

Part of the answer today can probably be summed up in one word: Miami. If you accept that old adage about politicians and reporters, "Call me anything but just spell my name right," Castro couldn't hire an agent to do what Miami does for him. Miami makes sure Washington doesn't forget Fidel.

The rest of the answer, if I am correct, is that Fidel Castro thinks about his international image all the time and works at keeping it on as many front pages as he can manage. He has no doubt whatsoever that he is always front-page news. Two separate conversations brought me to this conclusion.

The first was a conversation I had about Castro with the Italian journalist Oriana Fallaci. The occasion was when Sue and I were in Santiago de Cuba for the 25th anniversary celebrations of Castro's revolution. The night before the big speech, we were in the hotel bar along with the other dips and the foreign press corps. Somehow I ended up talking with Oriana. Sue says Oriana had other interests, but in fact all she was doing was pumping me, as any journalist would.

At some point in this conversation I must have asked Oriana what her schedule was. She replied that she really had none. She wanted an interview with Castro, which had not yet been granted, so she was trying to position herself where she would run across him and badger him for that interview. And she had actually had some success in that regard, for she had had a chance to speak to Castro that day at a noon reception for the press.

As I recall what she told me, she went up to Castro and said, "You probably don't know me..." To which Castro reportedly replied without hesitation, "Oh, but I do, you're the famous Italian journalist Oriana Fallaci." Grabbing that opening, she told me that she made her pitch: "Well, then, you may also know that your press office has been stonewalling me. I've requested an interview with you every day since I arrived in Cuba, but the answer is always a runaround. Tell your flunkies to act grown up and set a time for an interview." At this point, according to Oriana, Castro stepped back, looked her over, bellowed a laugh, and declared, "After what you did to Henry?"

Castro's reference was to Oriana's published interview with Henry Kissinger about ten years before. She had reported Kissinger describing himself as the Lone Ranger riding off in solitary pursuit of the bad guys. Whether she had betrayed a confidence, I don't know, but Kissinger was furious and the cognoscenti Inside the Beltway laughed for weeks.

My first reaction to that anecdote was to Castro's use of Kissinger's first name. They may be adversaries but Fidel saw himself as standing shoulder to shoulder with "Henry." Beyond the equality that that rejoinder conveys, there is also a definite feeling of empathy. It is as if Castro were complaining, "Why should we who shape the course of world events have to put up with the likes of you?"

I don't think it is too great a stretch to draw from that single sentence rejoinder the conclusion that Fidel Castro naturally assumes that he is front-page material. But even more than offering an insight into Castro's famous ego, Oriana's tale suggests how well Castro prepares himself to burnish and defend his international image. He not only made certain he knew which foreign journalists were in Santiago, in Oriana's case he reviewed her record, read (or reread) the Kissinger interview, and had given instructions to deny her an interview. Castro was not about to risk his image with a journalist that had committed lese-majesty with his colleague, Henry.

So I've concluded that Castro is still recognized today because he works at his image. But of course there are different degrees of recognition. We ail recognize Castro but we "Inside the Beltway" pay particular attention even long after Castro has faded into the bush leagues because he so successfully matched wits with us for so long. Frustration has conditioned us to pay attention. And then for us there is the Miami factor. But I'm not certain, if you broaden the definition, that the attention "we Americans" pay today goes beyond surface recognition. However, I also doubt that Castro understands the difference between the two "we"s. My last one-on-one-conversation with Castro both lent first-hand confirmation to the conclusions I drew from Oriana Fallaci's tale and revealed how little Castro understands that the substance of his image among the broader American public has hollowed out.

Toward the end of 1984 Washington conducted unpublicized migration negotiations with the Cuban Government. We sought to return to Cuba the criminals and the mentally ill whom Castro had sent with the tens of thousands of Cubans who fled the island on the so-called Mariel boat lift. That was when Castro, in a fit of pique at domestic dissidents, declared that anyone unhappy with the Revolution could leave, provided that he could get across the Gulf Stream to Florida. And so the Miami Cubans sent scores of boats to the port of Mariel to pick up anyone who just might be unhappy. The response was positive, as you might say. It seemed that the entire population was on the road to Mariel. And when those boats got to Key West, we let the Cubans in. In fact, at first we welcomed them.

Castro became even more furious, reasoning in a convoluted way that his black eye of dissidents, which was growing by the day, was all our fault. So he took the dregs of his prisons and the wretched of his mental institutions and put them on those boats from Miami. In essence he said, "Miami, if you want to take cousin Juanito, you've also got to take Chico the Con and Sara the Schizo." Well, Chico and Sara stood out like sore thumbs, and we took them right from the boats to our institutions. That was in 1980, and by 1984 we wanted to send Chico and Sara home. Obviously we had to give Castro something in return. What we did was stretch our immigration procedures. In effect, we gave him a safety valve for his dissidents by allowing more in legally.

For whatever reason, Castro had not told the Cuban public that he was negotiating this so-called migration agreement. But he couldn't keep it a secret indefinitely. So, when signature was put to paper and the White House released the text of the agreement, Castro too went public. I had been told by the Department about when the text would be released, of course, and thus was not surprised when the Cuban media announced that Castro would make a major address to the nation that evening. Coincidentally, Castro was hosting a reception for a visiting head of state that same evening that would begin a half hour later. I couldn't hear the address and also be on time for the reception, so I decided to be late. I was curious about how he would justify an agreement with us, so curious that I didn't want to wait until the next day to read it in the press.

Castro's speech was fascinating, because he didn't seem to know how to justify the agreement. It wasn't that he had difficulty justifying taking Chico and Sara back in exchange for more immigration visas for his less-than-loyal supporters. It was that he didn't seem to know how to justify the fact that he had authorized any agreement with his Yankee enemy. He spoke in circles, and I soon lost him and decided to skip the rest of the speech and go to the reception.

Reading that speech afterwards, I saw that for Castro the problem seemed to be consistency. At that time, Castro had had 25 or 26 years to establish first premises, and the very first of those was "Yankee Go Home." He was now chipping away at those premises and worried that his audience wouldn't understand. It was obvious to me that Castro worked on the assumption that when he speaks, you listen. And more, you pay attention and think about what he says. I guess that such an assumption was not far fetched in Cuba where he had made himself the only story in town. But that assumption became really interesting when Castro let it govern his approach to foreign relations.

So Sue and I drove down to the Palace of the Revolution, arriving after the receiving line had disbanded. I always loved those receptions. Great Cuban food, great rum, and the opportunity to match wits with the New Socialist Man, when he could be dragged away from the buffet table that would be his last tasty meal until the next reception. It may seem surprising, but most of the second-tier Cuban elite did, in fact, live off their ration books, just like the average guy in the street. So they loved official receptions for foreign dignitaries, where the buffet tables groaned. But I also loved the layout. It was an unwitting takeoff on that silly book by Regis Debray, "Revolution within the Revolution." There was always a reception within the reception. Because everyone was equal but some were more equal than others, the A List invitees were invited into an inner sanctum where the scotch was Black Label rather than Red and the rum was seven years old rather than three.

Castro had noted that I had not passed through the receiving line and thus, when it disbanded and before he went into the inner sanctum, he gave instructions to his chief of protocol to keep an eye out for me and to bring me in to see him if and when I arrived.

"Ferch, the Comandante wants to talk to you." Arismende, the chief of protocol, was typecast for the role of an unctuous headwaiter. I shook his hand, offered a few inanities, then followed him, and at least figuratively wiped off the palm of my hand on my pants. We passed by the buffet in the inner sanctum, where the visiting chief of state and the Central Committee of the Cuban Communist Party were busily tearing apart a roast pig basted in sour orange sauce. My eyes and nose lingered, but we did not pause.

'This way, Ferch." Arismende ushered me into a room behind the inner sanctum. Castro was seated on a sofa. No one else was in the room. Castro rose, shook my hand and asked about Sue. He has a preference for blondes. Then he sat back down and patted the sofa next to him, by way of instruction to me. Arismende took a seat in the far corner of the room. He was not only unctuous, he knew his place.

Castro then leaned toward me, put his hand on my shoulder, and said, "Ferch, I want you to tell the American people that I made a moral commitment today when I signed that agreement. I take this very seriously." That was it—no preamble, no discussion of the terms of the agreement, no questions about implementation. Just a bottom-line instruction for me to tell my fellow citizens that Fidel Castro had made a moral commitment. So I had my instruction, but Castro apparently was not confident that I fully understood the immensity of it all, because he continued on with the same theme for the next 15 to 25 minutes. "The agreement with Reagan is a moral commitment. The American people must understand that I'm serious. Tell them." And on and on.

At one point, when he seemed to pause for breath, I tried to ask questions about next steps, problems he might see with implementation, I forget what else. I needn't have tried. Once his lungs were refilled, he returned to the theme, overriding my words with a hand wave of dismissal. Since I obviously had not been invited into the Presence to converse, I sat back and let questions fill my mind: "Who does this guy think he is? What is this obsession with the American people? Does he really think I can tell 200-plus-million people anything? OK, I'll tell my brother-in-law in Toledo, Ohio. But first I'll have to remind him who Fidel Castro is. 'Fidel? Oh, that guy with the beard and a cigar.' And, Comandante, my brother-in-law is a very well-read man." My thoughts went on like this while Castro droned on around his theme.

Finally Castro stood up, gave me a couple of cigars, slapped me on the back, and jerked a shoulder at Arismende. The headwaiter came out of his chair in the corner and adopted a stance that indicated I should follow him. Castro made a whisking motion with his hand, as if to send me on my mission to the American people.

Arismende ushered me through the inner sanctum. I eyed that roast pig again, but he wouldn't pause. Messengers apparently are not A List material. Back in the B List reception, I headed for the buffet and tried to salvage what I could of the rapidly diminishing remains of a fine selection of highly caloric, highly cholesterol-raising dishes. My diplomatic colleagues crowded around. Not one had failed to note my summons to the inner sanctum and they sought material for tomorrow's cables. But my diplomatic armor held, soon I was able to catch Sue's eye, and we headed for the door.

Sue was brimming with curiosity, too, but she knew conversation would have to wait. We didn't have a technical security specialist on the staff, so we had to assume our car and residence were bugged. Thus, when we reached the residence and I said, "Why don't you get your swimsuit and pour yourself a drink," she knew what I meant and didn't hesitate. No one, not even the Cubans, could bug seven acres of tropical garden and an Olympic-size swimming pool.

Walking out through that garden, under the royal palms, the flame trees, the frangipanis, with bougainvillea and hibiscus on all sides, I thought still again, "Fidel or no Fidel, we're going to miss this." But then that one-sided conversation forced its way back into my mind.

When we reached the pool, I turned on the under-water lights, and Sue and I walked down the steps into the shallow end. Holding our drinks above water, we edged down the center until the water was neck high. Sue could wait no longer: "OK, what did the Great Man say? You were in there almost a half hour."

I took a sip of my rum and told her that it wasn't so much what he said as what he must have been thinking when he said it. "I think I just saw Fidel Castro as he sees himself. The closest analogy is Mount Rushmore. He thought he was talking policy, but it was really psychology. Let me give you the details and then you give me a laywoman's interpretation."

After I finished, she thought a bit and then said, "That was really bizarre. I think you need more than the help of a laywoman to figure him out."

With that, we finished our drinks, climbed out of the pool and walked back to the residence. It was quite late by then, so we turned in.

I fell asleep, as I always do, but Fidel Castro was still galloping around my mind shouting a message to the American people. That does not make for a restful night. I woke up at 3:30 and decided I would start drafting my report on the conversation then and there. I knew that I wasn't going to get back to sleep.

From the beginning of my conversation with Castro, it was clear to me that there was little of political substance and interest in what he was saying. OK, he was serious about the agreement. But we were too and we wouldn't have signed it if we thought that he was going to renege. No, what would really interest Washington was if I could use the conversation to interpret Fidel Castro, to contribute to an understanding of what makes him tick. And that meant I'd have to play psychologist.

So I went downstairs to the library and began looking up in the Oxford English Dictionary all the psychological terms I could remember. Admittedly, there weren't all that many, and it wasn't too long before I settled on "megalomania." There it was: "delusions of greatness," "an obsession with doing extravagant or grand things." If an intention to communicate with the "American people" wasn't an "extravagant thing" and "delusional," what else would it be, given Castro's humble status as a world mover and shaker? I began my drafting by placing those definitions as headers to the opening paragraph.

But almost immediately my analysis stalled. Sure, Fidel was delusional, but why in his own mind did he think that the "American people" would be interested in hearing from him? As I mulled over this question, I began to pull up from my memory images of Castro in action: at the Bay of Pigs rushing to the front and manning the cannon that allegedly sank one of the invading ships; at countless hours of long harangues of the Revolutionary Faithful, striding the stage making patented gestures and carefully reaching a crescendo of revolutionary emotion. Those were the images of a consummate actor who was accustomed to dominating the stage. And Castro the actor not only dominated the Cuban stage from those early guerrilla days in the Sierra Madre but soon after became a world-class thespian. The Cuban Missile Crisis; the alliance with the Soviets and the declaration that Cuba was a communist state; the support for guerrillas everywhere. Who could forget those theatrical extravaganzas? Certainly Castro couldn't forget them. So, as I began drafting again I postulated that Castro still sees himself striding the world stage, that for him nothing had changed during the previous decade.

World-class actors don't play in Bridgeport, of course. They demand world-class audiences. And who is the most important world-class audience? Why, it's the American people, of course. And they, understandably, are only interested in world-class actors. As I drafted I saw that I was becoming a bit extravagant myself. I considered toning down some of the language. But I was confident that I was on to something, and I didn't want my draft to be another routine Foreign Service cable. So I let the language stand.

Castro, the world-class actor, had no doubt, I wrote, that the world-class audience, the American people, recognized his importance. The relationship was one of equals. Given that relationship, it was only natural for Castro to assume that his equals were as interested in him as he was in them. And since he was frankly surprised that he had entered into an agreement, any agreement, with the Reagan Administration, I wrote that he had no doubt that the American people must also be surprised. Their surprise had to be met with an explanation. Thus his insistence that I tell the American people that he viewed the new agreement to be a "moral commitment," that it was not just another tactical maneuver in the decades-long duel between equals.

I suspected that my conclusion that history had distorted the lenses through which Castro views the world was not a totally original thought. But I hoped also that my personalized tale about how I reached this conclusion would give it both flavor and credibility. Apparently it did.

Some years later I learned that the psychiatrists at the CIA largely agreed with my analysis and reportedly used it in their own work. Hearing that would please any amateur psychologist.

For the record, while I didn't relay Castro's message to the American people, I did tell this tale to my brother-in-law in Toledo. After all he had been a participant in the conversation, at least in my thoughts, while Castro had instructed me. Mildly amused, my brother-in-law said he would pass the message along to any one in Toledo who might want to discuss the migration agreement. That was 16 years ago and he is still waiting.

Career Snapshot: Introduction to Honduras

Honduras is the least developed of the Central American countries, and probably has the least potential to develop. And yet while I served there as ambassador in the mid 1980s it was very close to the center of American foreign policy concerns. Those concerns ultimately put me at odds with the Administration and thus Honduras was to be my last assignment in the Foreign Service. Yet it too offered opportunities for service for which I am still grateful.

Chapter Thirteen

Why employ intelligent and highly paid ambassadors and then go and do their work for them? You don't buy a canary and sing yourself.

Alexander Douglas-Home

There probably aren't many jobs that give you the satisfaction of formulating and carrying out policies that further the national interest. The Foreign Service offers that satisfaction, especially as one rises to senior ranks. Perhaps the greatest challenge, and hence the greatest satisfaction, occurs during fast breaking events when there is no time to consult with Washington and debate what ought to be done. In such events an ambassador is largely on his or her own. I say largely because he or she will have contingent policies that were developed through rather rigorous exercises in which attempts are made to look ahead and mesh specific national interests with specific challenges and appropriate policy responses. The results of these exercises are approved at very high levels in the Department. Quite often we get it right and an ambassador takes appropriate action to meet a crisis and everyone applauds. But not always. What I found frustrating as I rose toward higher rank were those occasions when Washington did not support, or agreed only reluctantly to support, an ambassador who acted on predetermined policy guidelines.

Predetermined policy guidelines are often overtaken by changing circumstances and thus should not be followed blindly, of course. The frustration I refer to stemmed in my experience not from wholly different circumstances but from the emergence of competing policy agendas within the Administration. The Cold War abounded with such competing agendas, especially during the Reagan Administration, but the problem has deep roots.

I believe that the rationale for our policy during the Cold War gradually changed from primarily containment of Soviet expansion to containment plus the promotion of democratic values. We talked about defending Western democracies from the beginning but we also lived comfortably during the '40s and '50s with "our bastards," the Trujillos, the Batistas, the Somozas of my part of the world. With Kennedy, however, our policy became more value-oriented. Containment, or perhaps better said, a defensive posture, was never dropped, however. So falling "dominoes" jostled with "emerging democracies" for our attention right up to the end of the Cold War.

By the time I was sent as ambassador to Honduras, our stated policy was the strengthening of Honduran democracy while our less-publicized policy was the maintenance of Honduras as a base for supporting the "Contra" insurgents against the Cuban-supported Sandinista government in Nicaragua. The Democratic

Congress was all for the democracy policy, while the Reagan Administration was all for toppling the Sandinistas.

I arrived in Honduras just as a presidential campaign in that country was gearing up and just as our Congress was severely limiting what we could do to support the Contras. The Administration was apoplectic. Central America might be lost on their watch! And it *would* be lost if the Honduran government, sensitive to the congressional winds, told the Contras to get lost.

Initially I lived comfortably with both the stated "democracy" policy and support for the Contras. Neither seemed to threaten the other. Admittedly, my recent experience in Cuba had made me a bit doubtful about the long-term nature of the Sandinista threat in Central America. During my last months in Havana a major Soviet economic mission visited and read Castro the riot act. I reported that the Soviets bluntly told Castro that the free lunch was over. Since the support the Sandinistas received from the Cubans ultimately depended on Cuba's Soviet supply line, I foresaw that the Sandinistas would have difficulty surviving in Nicaragua, much less toppling dominoes elsewhere in Central America. The Contras might hasten the process but I doubted that they would be the crucial factor. Washington didn't see it that way, of course, and I did not push the argument. I had already made it in Havana and hadn't provoked much of a reaction. For many in Washington, the Soviets and their allies remained ten feet tall until the Berlin Wall fell on them.

The situation was tailor-made for the Honduran president. He voiced support for democracy but he was also keenly aware that Washington needed Honduras as a base. The Honduran constitution told him he couldn't run for president again, but Honduras has had a lot of constitutions. And he rather liked being president. So it wasn't long before I began to pick up political rumors about an impending constitutional amendment.

Next, the president invited me to lunch with a couple of his military aides. The campaign for president was then in full swing. Asking for my opinions about the candidates, which I sidestepped, the aides began to give me their opinions, with an emphasis on how wishy-washy all of them were on the Contras. When I tried to turn the conversation to the government's development programs, the president kicked the ball back to the weakness of all the candidates—weakness on the subject of the Contras, that is. It was all less than subtle, but I didn't bite until dessert. I then declared that I wanted to speak as clearly as possible. Looking straight at the president, I declared that it was the policy of the U.S. Government to support the coming Honduran electoral process. And that ended the conversation. I reported the conversation but never got any reaction from Washington.

Then I learned that a White House official visited Honduras to meet with the president without my knowledge. I heard it from an American reporter. The second policy agenda was emerging and the Honduran president was playing to it, but it was all a bit blurry to me at the time.

At this point I probably should have flown to Washington and hashed out our policy priorities. But at that time the emergence of the second agenda was not as clear-cut to me as it now is looking back. Furthermore, our policy was to support the electoral process, and the assistant secretary had signed off on that policy. I thought that I had my marching orders. But perhaps more to the point, I approved of them. This was my third Central American assignment, and I had long come to the conclusion that that little backwater deserved better from us than what it usually got.

I was probably also influenced by a somewhat similar incident that had occurred when I was serving in Guatemala some ten year before. At that time I had persuaded the ambassador to include in a contingent policy exercise the recommendation that, if the Guatemalan military staged a coup to prevent the next elections, we would terminate economic assistance. (My recommendation was not based on foresight. Coups were the norm in Guatemala, elections the exception.) The ambassador accepted my recommendation and Washington signed off on the contingent policy. Of course the Guatemalan military staged their coup and, again of course, Washington backed down. Most Guatemalans probably didn't give the situation much thought, it was the norm after all, but it did influence me.

So I was not enthusiastic about cooperating with the Honduran president's efforts to set aside his constitution. In any event, developments occurred too quickly for lengthy discussions with Washington even if I had flown up to hash things out. And that is the point of this tale.

It wasn't long after I had heard that someone from Washington had met with the Honduran president that the president made his move. It was morning, and I was in my office when my secretary stuck her head through the door to say that the speaker of the Honduran Congress was in the waiting room and wanted to speak with me right away. She said that he was very agitated.

I went out to meet him and ushered him into my office. He was agitated; in fact, he was sweating. He even turned down my offer of coffee and got right to the point, which is not a Honduran characteristic. "Mr. Ambassador," he said, "you've got to do something. You have got to stop him."

He went on like this for at least a minute before I could calm him down and pull the story out of him. He explained that the president had just called him with instructions to convene a special session of the Congress for that afternoon to consider a draft law that would postpone the elections for two years. During that time the president would stay in office, of course. The speaker was opposed to the proposed law but didn't seem to know what to do. He kept saying that I had to do something.

My first reaction was very negative. I told him that Honduras was his country, that if anyone should do something it should be he. I then gave him both barrels; I clearly was losing my diplomatic imperturbability. "The problem with Central America and much of the rest of Latin America is that you always expect that the gringos will bail you out. Just vote against the president!"

I should have spared myself that breach of professionalism. I don't think he even heard me, because he continued moaning and groaning about what the president was going to do. Since I clearly wasn't stiffening his backbone, my thoughts finally went to our stated policy. If I was going to follow it, the moment was now, even if it meant more intervention. So I told the speaker I'd think about it. He clearly was hopeless, so there was no use in bringing him into my plans.

As soon as the speaker left, I called in the press attaché and told him about my conversation. I asked him what he thought about an interview on air with a radio reporter. The reporter would seemingly take the initiative by calling me and asking what I thought about the proposed law. We would suggest the questions so that the interview would hit the target. The press attaché liked the idea and we drafted the questions then and there, and he ran out to telephone the radio station.

I then telephoned the Department to tell them what I was about to do. There was no time for anyone in the Department to consider my initiative as a proposal and, in any event, I probably was already committed, but I wanted them to know. I hadn't expected any opposition to my initiative; our policy was quite clear. Maybe I even hoped for a few congratulatory words about my creativity. So I was taken aback when the Deputy Assistant Secretary said, "Well, it's on your head, John."

He may have said a bit more, but that was the essence of the conversation, and he hung up. If I hadn't seen the second agenda clearly before, I did then. So my eyes were finally opened wide. We had a policy of supporting democracy in Honduras, but don't let that policy jeopardize our efforts to topple the Sandinistas!

Now, I was no fan of the Sandinistas. I hadn't liked much of what I had seen in Cuba, and it seemed pretty clear to me that the Sandinistas were planning to implant Castro's system in Nicaragua. Nicaraguans deserved better. But Hondurans also deserved better than being given the bill for our Cold War policies. And perhaps more to the point at that moment, I gradually became royally teed off at how I had just been treated by the Deputy Assistant Secretary. Rather than work with me in support of our policy, he was setting me up as scapegoat if a thwarted Honduran president turned on the Contras.

Such thoughts were reaching a crescendo when my secretary stuck her head in again and said that the radio reporter was on the phone. So I was primed to give the charade of an interview a very real dollop of emotion.

The reporter played his lines beautifully: "Mr. Ambassador, there are rumors circulating throughout Tegucigalpa that the president will propose this afternoon that the elections be postponed two years. I am certain that our many listeners will be interested in your views and the views of your government about a postponement of presidential elections."

I responded, script in hand: "Well, first, let me say that while I am aware of the rumors, I cannot believe that there is any truth behind them. I know the president well, he is a sincere democrat, and he has told me that his highest goal in these last months of his presidency is to conduct open and fair elections and turn over the sash of office to his constitutionally elected successor."

You know, as I said that mouthful, I am almost certain that I was also recalling that famous quote by Henry Wotton, the quote that every new foreign service officer learns: "An ambassador is an honest man sent to lie abroad for the good of his country." If I didn't recall it then I did soon afterwards.

The reporter turned to the second question we had given him. "If, however, Mr. Ambassador, the elections were to be postponed, what would be the reaction of the American Government?"

Speaking with what I thought was a professorially grave voice, I replied, "That is a hypothetical question which I won't answer. Honduras is a sovereign country and will conduct its political process as it sees fit. What I can say is that, with regard to the American political process, the government, all political parties, and all citizens are firmly committed to our constitution. Our strength is that we support and defend that constitution and do not arbitrarily depart from it."

It was probably fortunate that that was the last of the questions the press attaché had given the reporter and that he therefore signed off at that point for I was getting really wound up and might have departed from the script. I might even have subjected those Honduran listeners to my translation of the Gettysburg Address. Or maybe that would have been a good thing. For although I now know that a lot of listeners heard the message loud and clear, one did not.

In about an hour the speaker of the Congress called again, more frantic than before, and cried that the president was going ahead with the special session and his draft law. He pleaded with me to come to the Congress and "Stop him!" I finally calmed him down and told him that I would think about it. Which I did. And I didn't get very far. If the president was determined to push his law through there obviously wasn't anything that I could do. But in Honduran eyes I was a player now so I couldn't simply ignore his move.

Acting on the principle that if you don't know what to do, you can at least appear to be doing something, I decided to go to the Congress and sit in the visitors' gallery and await developments. Perhaps after all those years in Latin America by now I was also a bit of a macho. I wasn't going to ignore the president's challenge.

At the Congress Honduran politicians and hangers-on were milling about, and they all saw me. So it wasn't long before a TV reporter shuffled across the aisle to where I was sitting and asked if he could interview me. I couldn't turn him down, because I had spoken on radio, nor did I want to. But I didn't have any new arguments to make, either.

For better lighting, the reporter took me out on a balcony. As the camera crew was setting up, I looked down at the plaza in front of the Congress building. A fairly large crowd had gathered. Some were shouting, "Elecciones, Sí!" Pretty soon the entire two or three hundred people in the crowd had taken up that chant. When the reporter said that he was ready he placed me, for visual effect, I suppose, next to the railing, and began.

"Mr. Ambassador, our president has called Congress into session. Although he hasn't arrived yet, his advisers say that he will propose postponing the elections for two years. I heard you on the radio this morning. The situation is not hypothetical now. So what is your view about the president's attempt to postpone the elections?"

He was right; it wasn't hypothetical. The president was about to stage a coup, albeit with the cover of what was probably an unconstitutional law, which was no obstacle for him because the Honduran Supreme Court had the clout of a justice of the peace. And I guessed that he believed Washington would go along. I wondered what that special emissary had told him. So what could I say that would sway him?

Looking at the crowd milling around below, the idea came to me. I'd appeal over his head. So I put on a serious face, turned to the camera and, with my right arm pointed over the railing at the crowd, declared in a tone that I hoped was both serious and ironic: "As a diplomat, I am a professional observer. And it seems to me"—here I paused, turned and looked at the crowd and then slowly turned back—"that the

Honduran people are more enthusiastic about elections even than the North Americans. If the elections aren't held the Honduran people are going to be very frustrated."

That TV interview was also live. Afterward I stayed on the balcony and chatted with the reporter. After about ten or fifteen minutes, he drew my attention to the crowd again. It had doubled, at least. After the fact we learned that the broadcast had been widely seen and that it had brought out the growing crowd.

I returned to my seat. The president still had not arrived. I waited about forty-five minutes. Congressmen started drifting away. I cornered a couple of them. They expressed the opinion that the president wouldn't show up, that he was backing down. They were right. So eventually I returned to the embassy and sent a reporting cable to the Department.

The Department never commented on that cable, on my intervention, or on the fact that the president dropped his proposal to postpone the elections. Friends in the Department later conjectured that my superiors were waiting for the president to drop the other shoe and take out his frustration on the Contras. He didn't do that, however. The elections were held and the new, honestly elected president took office some months later. Ironically, the newly elected president, concluding that my action had made possible his election, gave his full support to the Contras, although during the campaign he had expressed grave concern about the threat the Contras posed to Honduras.

No one in Washington ever acknowledged that irony to me. While I would have welcomed some recognition from Washington that I had successfully pursued our stated policy and ensured that elections were held, such recognition did come from many sectors in Honduras. But Hondurans didn't comment on the other side of that coin. An American had once again intervened in internal Honduran politics. So while the Administration might have had conflicting policy agendas, I was guilty of placing objective and tactics in conflict. The practice of diplomacy is often that messy.

Career Snapshot: And How It Ended

Throughout almost all my career I worked for superiors who were truly remarkable men (no women then). They were both career officers and political appointees, and the latter, obvious in a career spanning thirty-one years, were stalwarts of both political parties. I learned from all of them, many became my personal friends, and most went far out of their way to advance my career. I look back on them fondly and with admiration. My career did not end on such notes, however, and in any collection of tales from the Foreign Service, that ending also must be told.

I arrived in Honduras in midsummer 1985, after Congress had authorized so-called "humanitarian assistance" for the Contras but continued its prohibition on lethal aid. Butter but no guns, you might say. Since you can't fight a war with butter, the fervent Cold Warriors in the Administration sought ways to circumvent the congressional prohibition. Money was found and illegal arms shipments were made. Now, Honduras was the original Banana Republic, with all that term implies. Such arms shipments couldn't be kept secret for long, and they knew it. If I stumbled on the secret and reported it, Congress and the press would not be far behind. So they concluded that I would have to be on board. But first they had to "prepare" me. I was summoned to Washington, and in a one-on-one, the Assistant Secretary, my boss, accused me of not supporting the Administration. No specifics, no response to my requests for examples. I could feel my blood pressure rising and thought, "This is McCarthyism!" Finally I cut through his innuendo and said, "I support this Administration like I've supported all Administrations since Eisenhower. I'm a professional." And he replied, "OK, I accept that. Come to a meeting in my office tomorrow at 10:00."

There were four of them, all subsequently infamous during the Congressional hearings on the Iran-Contra Affair. They represented Defense, CIA and the White House, as well as State. They were the men who ran the Contra war. The conversation that ensued was as indirect as that with my boss the previous night, but just as clear. They wanted me to volunteer to take responsibility for all aspects of the Contra program in Honduras. I remember thinking, "If these guys were the cops I'd demand my lawyer." But the "cop" was my boss, and there was no lawyer to call. So I bobbed and weaved, and finally they grew tired and ended the meeting.

I returned to Tegucigalpa that evening both confused and alarmed. I couldn't turn to the Assistant Secretary for advice, because it was he who had put me on the spot. So after much reflection, I sent him a back-channel message that read: "I'm the ambassador and thus responsible for all United States Government programs in this country. So I'll be responsible for the Contras. But, I will feel more comfortable if you will give me my instructions in writing and I will respond in kind."

And so they removed me.

I still had a job but no career. I thought to out-wait them by treading water until the next elections. I was an apolitical professional but I rather hoped that if the Democrats won the White House I might return to the career. I was quite irritated, of course, and told senior management that I wouldn't work during the meantime in the Department. They apparently did not want to make an issue of it and when friends suggested that I talk with Senator Bill Bradley, the Department detailed me to his office. The elections came and the Republicans stayed in the White House. I asked senior management to inquire whether I was persona non grata with the new Republican Administration and was told that I was. So I retired.

I had no regrets then and have none now. I had had a wonderful career and I knew that I would do it all over again even if I could foresee the ending. But real satisfaction didn't come until the Iran-Contra Scandal unfolded and my son said, "If you hadn't done that, Dad, I wouldn't be speaking to you now."

Postscript

Compliments can come in many guises. During my last months in Honduras the new president told me that he had sent one of his advisors to Cuba to try to determine Cuban policy in Central America. The advisor met with Castro and during that conversation asked Castro if he personally knew me. Castro said that he did and then said that I was "Muy inteligente pero peligroso." "Very intelligent but dangerous." I've thought about his assessment many times in subsequent years and have laughed a lot but can't begin to guess what led Castro to that conclusion.

About the Author

Ambassador John Ferch is from Toledo, Ohio, and attended Princeton University, graduating Phi Beta Kappa, with honors. He subsequently studied at the University of Michigan and the National War College. Upon graduation from Princeton he entered the Foreign Service and was posted to Buenos Aires, beginning eight postings in Latin America. Through his early career he served as an economist. He concluded his service as Deputy Chief of Mission in Mexico, Chief of the United States Interest Section in Havana, and Ambassador to Honduras. He is married to Sue McMurray. They have four children and three grandchildren. Ambassador Ferch is a collector of Latin American contemporary and folk art and is an accomplished carpenter.

About Miniver Press

Miniver Press is a publisher of lively and informative non-fiction e- and print books, with titles covering history, politics, business, music, sports, biography, memoir, and performing arts. For more information, contact editor@miniverpress.com

www.ingramcontent.com/pod-product-compliance
Lightning Source LLC
Chambersburg PA
CBHW060749050426
42449CB00008B/1333

* 9 7 8 1 9 3 9 2 8 2 3 2 3 *